P9-DTQ-343

CAPITALISM

A GRAPHIC GUIDE

DAN CRYAN
SHARRON SHATIL
& PIERO

This edition published in the UK and the USA in 2019 by Icon Books Ltd, Omnibus Business Centre, 39-41 North Road, London N7 9DP email: info@iconbooks.com www.iconbooks.com

Sold in the UK, Europe and Asia by Faber & Faber Ltd, Bloomsbury House, 74–77 Great Russell Street, London WC1B 3DA or their agents

Distributed in the UK, Europe and Asia by Grantham Book Services, Trent Road, Grantham, NG31 7XQ

Distributed in the USA by Publishers Group West, 1700 Fourth Street, Berkeley, CA 94710

Distributed in Canada by Publishers Group Canada, 76 Stafford Street, Unit 300, Toronto, Ontario M6J 2S1

Distributed in Australia and New Zealand by Allen & Unwin Pty Ltd, PO Box 8500, 83 Alexander Street, Crows Nest, NSW 2065

Distributed in South Africa by Jonathan Ball, Office B4, The District, 41 Sir Lowry Road, Woodstock 7925

Distributed in India by Penguin Books India, 7th Floor, Infinity Tower – C, DLF Cyber City, Gurgaon 122002, Haryana

ISBN: 978-178578-514-6

Text and illustrations copyright © 2013, 2019 Icon Books Ltd

The author and artist have asserted their moral rights.

Edited by Duncan Heath and Kiera Jamison

No part of this book may be reproduced in any form, or by any means, without prior permission in writing from the publisher.

Printed by Clays Ltd, Elcograf S.p.A.

Capital and Capitalism

Capitalism is the name of a family of economic systems based on the private ownership of the means of production and trading goods for profit. Capitalist economies tend to be characterized by free competition and industrialization, although capitalism without industry is not a contradiction in terms.

Broadly speaking, capitalist systems give a central role to the accumulation of resources that can be used for further production. These resources, known as "**capital**", give capitalism its name.

Capitalism vs. Feudalism

Once it had taken hold in Europe, capitalism spread around the world like wildfire, the driving force behind business, prosperity, empire and exploitation. As capitalism is an economic system based on trade, private ownership, and currency, its development is bound up with the history of trade and banking.

The food-supplying landowners became the nobility. The feudal economic system they constructed was based on a careful balance between small land units and a stable level of production. Feudalism aims for stability, and this makes it diametrically opposed to capitalism with its search for ever-growing markets.

The Crusades

While merchants and artisans, such as bakers and weavers, had begun to develop influence in Europe's cities, it was the Church that gave rise to what was effectively medieval Europe's first great international trade venture – the Crusades, which started in 1095.

The Crusades led to conquests along the eastern rim of the Mediterranean and gave Europeans more control over traditional trade routes. As a result, the kingdoms of Europe found themselves shipping goods and people across relatively long distances for the first time since the days of the Roman Empire.

The rise of trade and banking in 14th-century Europe eventually became the **Renaissance**, which was supported by bankers made princes like the Medici.

AS THE ITALIAN MERCHANT CLASS GREW RICHER, THEY GAINED POWER AND INFLUENCE. THIS PLAYED A SIGNIFICANT ROLE IN THE DEVELOPMENT OF REPUBLICAN CITY-STATES LIKE GENOA AND SIENA.

Lorenzo De'Medici
(1449–92)

HOWEVER, THE SCALE OF ITALIAN TRADE WAS TOO SMALL AND LOCAL TO SHAKE THE FOUNDATIONS OF FEUDALISM BEYOND A FEW TOWNS.

The Knights Templar

The first commercial banks appeared in the late 13th century in Italian towns like Siena. The word comes from *banco* – Italian for bench – since at first banking services were provided on benches at the town's centre. But banking does not begin with the Italian merchants – its origins lie with the Knights Templar, an order of warrior monks founded in 1096 to ensure the safe passage of European pilgrims heading to Jerusalem in the aftermath of the First Crusade.

THE JOURNEY BACK AND FORTH FROM EUROPE TO BYZANTIUM AND BEYOND WASN'T EASY.

BANDITS AND PIRATES LURKED ALONG THE WAY AND DISEASE COULD STRIKE UNPREDICTABLY.

So when an order of hardened, experienced Crusaders, who were also known for being zealously honest, offered to take the risk of the journey upon themselves, many jumped at the offer.

The Templars soon had representatives in all the major cities of Europe, and held a series of forts along the main roads connecting the Crusader states.

That allowed people to travel light and fast, and to buy what they needed locally wherever they got to. They would need to part with only a small percentage of their gold as a service charge.

Dissolution of the Templars

The Templars got immensely rich during the heyday of the Crusades. Because they were so vital to the survival of the Crusader states, they were granted permission by the Pope to run their own affairs, which meant they were effectively answerable to no one. As the Crusader states began to flounder, the Templars invested more and more of their vast wealth in property in Europe.

AS THE MIDDLE EASTERN VENTURE APPROACHED ITS DEMISE, THE LEADERS OF EUROPE GREW INCREASINGLY UNCOMFORTABLE WITH US HOLDING A FORTUNE THEY COULDN'T GET THEIR HANDS ON.

FRANCE, FOR EXAMPLE, GOT SO INVOLVED IN THE CRUSADES THAT MOST OF THE KING'S TREASURY WAS SITTING IN OUR "TEMPLE" IN PARIS.

> EVENTUALLY CHURCH AND STATE UNITED AGAINST US, AND WE WERE ACCUSED OF HERESY AND THE PERFORMANCE OF UNSPEAKABLE ACTS.

The order was dissolved in 1314, its leaders were put to the stake, and its wealth confiscated and divided up. The Pope entrusted his share to other Knightly orders that were not so independent. It ended up funding such ventures as the conquest of Prussia from its pagan natives and the reconquest of Spanish territory from the Arabs.

Banking lived on and developed mainly in Italy by private hands, but its basic idea remained unchanged from the days of the Templars to the arrival of the Rothschilds in the 19th century (see page 48).

Opening up the Trade Routes

By the end of the 15th century, improvements in the design of ships and inventions like the clock and the compass meant that crossing the ocean became feasible.

The newly formed Christian kingdoms of Spain and Portugal saw it worthwhile to send Columbus westward and Vasco da Gama southward in search of a naval route to India that would bypass the Muslim-dominated land routes.

Spain and Portugal found themselves suddenly with trading options all along the African and Asian coasts, as well as vast and rich new territories in the New World. From the 16th century onwards, international trade offered prospects of wealth far superior to the grain produced by the small feudal fiefs of Europe. With the arrival of that wealth, the feudal system faded away and was replaced by what came to be known later as a **mercantile economy**.

ROUGHLY SPEAKING, A MERCANTILE ECONOMY IS BASED ON THE IDEA THAT THE AMOUNT OF WEALTH OF A COUNTRY IS REPRESENTED BY THE OVERALL PROFIT IT MAKES FROM TRADE.

EACH STRIP OF LAND HAS A LIMITED AMOUNT OF TRADEABLE RESOURCES. SO THE VOLUME OF A COUNTRY'S TRADE DEPENDS ON THE AMOUNT OF LAND OVER WHICH IT HAS TRADE RIGHTS.

13

Expansionism

The rise in trade led to expansionism, and any European power that could afford it would send off ships, hoping to find new territory that "no one" (i.e. no other European) had discovered yet. Controlling land overseas gave these Europeans access to resources that could be exploited, often at the cost of the local inhabitants.

The transition to a mercantile economy also played a major role in the formation of the modern state out of the loose array of feudal estates.

CUSTOMARILY THE MONARCH HELD CLAIM TO THE NEW TERRITORIES OVERSEAS, AND THEIR MANAGEMENT REQUIRED A LARGE ADMINISTRATIVE BODY UNDER DIRECT ROYAL CONTROL.

THIS WAS THE FIRST ANCESTOR OF NATIONAL GOVERNMENT.

SERVING THE KING IN TIMES OF WAR HAD BEEN PROFITABLE THROUGHOUT THE MIDDLE AGES, BUT WITH TERRITORIAL EXPANSION, SERVING THE KING ABROAD BECAME A FAR MORE LUCRATIVE PROSPECT FOR THE NOBILITY THAN MANAGING THEIR PRIVATE ESTATES.

...ch merchants could also be knighted and accepted to the king's ...vice. In this way, the king's government reinforced its position as ...in avenue of social, political and financial advance.

...ile a powerful, centralized monarchy created the first great Euro... ...pires, it held back the development of a strong and independen... ...rchant class, and that held back private enterprise. As a result, ...pitalism did not grow out of the empires of Spain and Portugal, ... of the disadvantaged newcomers to the race for international ...d especially England and the Netherlands.

The Birthplace of Capitalism

The Netherlands is a small nation but its contribution to the development of capitalism is immense.

It may be said that the Dutch created the only true European "empire of trade" and never joined in the imperialist land grab that happened after the Industrial Revolution.

The Dutch held the chain of islands in the Indian ocean now known as Indonesia, and a few small bases in the Caribbean, but their trading posts spanned the globe in the 17th and 18th centuries.

Amsterdam itself was the greatest trade city in Europe up to the Industrial Revolution, and was home to the first stock exchange and insurance company. The Netherlands is considered by many historians to be the first truly capitalist nation in the world.

The Dutch East India Company

The Dutch East India Company, formed in 1602, was one of the first multi-national companies. It was run like a partnership among the Dutch states. Each held an independent branch (called a "chamber"), but a directorate of seventeen members who represented each of the chambers decided the company's strategy on a yearly basis.

The East India Company created the Dutch empire in Indonesia by means of brute force combined with economic pressure. It managed to drive the Portuguese off most of their trade posts in the Indian Ocean. It was a success story of individual enterprise that was much imitated, and it stayed ahead of competition until the final decades of the 18th century.

English Pirates

Like the Netherlands, England was a Protestant country threatened by the Catholic might of Spain at sea and France on land. As things stood in the second half of the 16th century, the English crown had nothing to lose by encouraging private ship-owners to make a living out of pirating the slow and heavy Spanish merchant ships returning from South America laden with gold and silver.

BUT ENGLAND'S ECONOMIC AND POLITICAL PROGRESS WAS SLOW, AND EVEN THE WEATHER-FUELLED COLLAPSE OF THE SPANISH ARMADA IN 1588 DIDN'T STOP SPAIN BEING THE DOMINANT NAVAL POWER.

WE CONTINUED OUR LINE OF CROWN-SPONSORED PIRACY UNTIL IT WAS STOPPED, AT LEAST FOR A WHILE, BY THE END OF THE ANGLO-SPANISH WAR IN 1604.

The Power of Private Investment

Elizabeth I had founded the British East India Company by royal charter in 1600. During the time of her successor James I, England became well used to private companies financing government-sanctioned projects. With the Virginia Company (founded in 1606), James used private investment and the gap in hostilities with Spain to start Jamestown, Britain's first lasting colony in North America.

Hobbes, the First Capitalist Thinker

The first major thinker to put these new ideas down on paper was **Thomas Hobbes** (1588–1679). Hobbes was basically the first great capitalist philosopher. Unlike many of the political thinkers who came before him – who looked at questions like "What is justice?" or "Who should rule?" – Hobbes put the individual at the centre of political theory.

> FROM GALILEO I LEARNED OF THE SCIENTIFIC METHOD THAT TRIES TO LOOK FOR THE SIMPLEST BITS ...

> ... AND FROM THERE TO IMAGINE WHAT FORCES AND MOTIONS GENERATED BY THESE BITS ACCOUNT FOR THE THINGS THAT WE SEE.

So the correct method for political science is to start from an understanding of the things that compose society – i.e. people, their desires and temperament – and move on to an understanding of society as a whole.

The Power of the Individual

The type of person that Hobbes found was individualistic and "infinitely free", recognizing no bounds to their freedom. They live in fear of their own death and were born into the world with the right to defend themselves and to do whatever is required to preserve their own life and to resist harm and imprisoment.

I UNDERSTAND A PERSON'S POWER AS THEIR ABILITY TO USE A PRESENT MEANS TO OBTAIN A FUTURE GOOD.

SO I CALL SOMEONE POWERFUL IF THEY CAN EASILY USE THINGS AVAILABLE TO THEM NOW TO DO WHAT THEY WANT IN THE FUTURE.

An individual's power is determined by many things such as their strength, intelligence, or social standing, all of which have a direct impact on their ability to do what they want to do. But it is not enough for an individual to be strong, or have a large circle of friends that they can call on to help them. Rather, that strength must be greater than other people's, as only then can one be sure of achieving one's goals.

> The Value or Worth of a man, is as of all other things, his Price; that is to say as much as would be given for the use of his Power: and therefore is not absolute; but a thing dependent on the judgement and need of another ... And as in other things, so in men, not the seller but the buyer determines the Price.

Hobbes, *Leviathan*, Chapter 10

It makes no sense to speak of the value of man like this unless it is possible for a man to trade his power, or work, for money. So it is that even before he got to analysing the state and how it should be structured, Hobbes thought of man in a capitalist framework.

The State of Nature

Hobbes took this view of mankind and imagined a time when there was no effective government. He thought that without strong government "the wickedness of bad men also compels good men to have recourse, for their own protection, to the virtues of war, which are violence and fraud". The result is that everyone battles with everyone else for every small advantage. It is, in effect, a war of all against all. Hobbes called this imagined pre-history the "state of nature".

Leviathan, Chapter 13

In such condition, there is no place for Industry; because the fruit thereof is uncertain; and consequently no Culture of the Earth; no Navigation, nor use of the commodities that may be imported by Sea; no commodious Building; no Instruments of moving, and removing such things as require much force; no Knowledge of the face of the Earth; no account of Time; no Arts; no Letters; no Society; and which is worst of all, continual fear, and danger of violent death; And the life of man, solitary, poore, nasty, brutish, and short.

Leviathan and the Social Contract

Rather than live in this anarchic hell, Hobbes thought that people subject themselves to the authority of a supreme ruler (which can either be an individual or a group of people), as that allows them to live happier, more prosperous lives – and he called this sovereign power "Leviathan". The relationship is supposed to be contractual – people trade their natural right to all things in exchange for a peaceful society.

IN PRACTICE, THINGS DON'T QUITE WORK OUT LIKE THIS. AT THE END OF MY MASTERPIECE *LEVIATHAN* (1651), I ADMIT THAT IN REALITY MOST STATES ARE PROBABLY FORCED ON THEIR INHABITANTS RATHER THAN AS THE RESULT OF MUTUAL AGREEMENT.

Hobbes became controversial in his 50s. In 1640 the political climate in England was tense, as the country edged towards civil war. It was then that Hobbes published a book on the necessity of a strong ruler. His views were unpopular with both sides, and so he left for France, where he became the tutor of Charles II while the future king was in exile.

Back in England, Hobbes never really escaped controversy. He survived Cromwell and was given a pension from Charles II when the monarchy was restored in 1660, only to find himself accused of heresy and banned from printing anything else on politics. He died in 1679 at the age of 90.

Natural Reason and Private Property

By the time Hobbes died, the Virginia Company had collapsed in 1624 and Virginia had become a colony under the rule of a crown-appointed governor. Charles I of England had been tried and beheaded in 1649. Government-sponsored piracy had come back into vogue in the Caribbean as privateers like Henry Morgan sailed the Spanish Main looking for gold and bounty.

And in England a genius called **John Locke** (1632–1704) took a different view of mankind in its natural state. To Locke, the state of nature was an idyll where man lived subject only to the laws of nature and the will of God.

UNLIKE HOBBES, I THINK THAT PEOPLE WOULD HAVE LIVED PEACEFULLY IN THE STATE OF NATURE.

THIS HARMONY COMES FROM THE FACT THAT IN THE STATE OF NATURE, MANKIND FOLLOWS MORAL RULES GIVEN TO HIM BY HIS FACULTY OF **NATURAL REASON.**

To back this up, Locke used the example, fresh from the colonies, of the Native Americans – believed to be, for the most part, living in peace close to nature.

Where Hobbes granted man control of his own labour, Locke went further, giving people the right to the fruits of their labour. He started from the idea that in the state of nature everything is commonly owned by all mankind, and asked how the ownership of **private property** was possible at all.

Locke's question is of fundamental importance to the moral justification of capitalism. If private property cannot be justified, then nor can trade or investment, as they are dependent on the idea that a person can own property and can, within reason, do with it what they want.

NATURAL REASON TELLS US THAT EVERYONE HAS THE RIGHT TO PRESERVE THEIR OWN BODY; IT FOLLOWS THAT PEOPLE HAVE THE RIGHT TO THE FOOD AND DRINK THEY NEED TO STAY ALIVE.

FROM THIS IT SEEMS THAT THERE MUST BE SOME FORM OF PRIVATE OWNERSHIP, AS THE FOOD I EAT BECOMES MINE AS IT LITERALLY BECOMES PART OF ME.

Labour = Ownership?

Locke thought that the thing that allows us to claim part of nature as our own is that we have somehow worked on it – in Locke's words, that we have "mixed our labour" with it. This is what allows the person who has gone to the effort to gather acorns from the forest to claim them as his own, or the farmer who has cultivated some land to claim it as his own.

The idea that people have natural rights to private property and to decide how and where they work became the bedrock of liberal capitalism. In liberal thought, if a person has a natural right to something, then no one, not even the state, can interfere with it.

As elegant as Locke's solution for a natural right to property is, it suffers from a significant flaw. This was pointed out in the 20th century by the American philosopher **Robert Nozick** (1938–2002).

I NOTICED THAT SIMPLY MIXING YOUR LABOUR WITH SOMETHING IS NOT ENOUGH TO MAKE IT YOURS. IF I WERE TO TAKE A CAN OF SOUP AND POUR IT INTO THE SEA I WOULD, ACCORDING TO LOCKE, HAVE MIXED MY LABOUR WITH IT.

BUT IT SEEMS ABSURD TO SAY THAT I NOW OWN THE SEA. RATHER, WHAT WE NEED IS SOMETHING ELSE, IN ADDITION TO ADDING WORK, TO CLAIM SOMETHING AS OUR OWN.

Unfortunately, neither Nozick nor anybody else has yet come up with a widely accepted account of what that something else is. Some say cultivation or enclosing is required, others that value must be added to the thing, others that no one else should be injured by the acquisition. But none of these suggestions is without problems.

Locke and Civil Government

Not only did Locke try to come up with an account of the justification for private property, he also proposed a structure for society that lends itself to capitalism. For Locke, the role of "civil government" is to protect the freedom and security of all members of society.

LIKE ME, LOCKE STARTED WITH MAN'S NATURAL RIGHTS (HIS RIGHT TO DEFEND HIMSELF, RIGHT TO PRIVATE PROPERTY, ETC.).

HE ALSO THOUGHT THAT A CONTRACT LAY AT THE ROOT OF SOCIETY.

HOWEVER, I BELIEVE THAT THE PURPOSE OF GOVERNMENT IS TO PROTECT THE INTERESTS OF ITS SUBJECTS.

Unlike Hobbes, Locke thought that a civil government should not wield absolute power. Instead, people should be free to replace any government that attempts to subject them to its absolute or arbitrary rule.

Locke and Colonialism

These ideas stood out in contrast to the tightly regulated way in which the British government was treating its colonies, so it's perhaps not surprising that after the American Revolution of 1775–83, Locke's ideas had a huge influence on the founding fathers – though Locke's attitude to colonial politics is somewhat more ambiguous.

Locke spent much of his life under the influence of Anthony Ashley Cooper, 1st **Earl of Shaftesbury** (1621–83). The two met when Shaftesbury came to Oxford looking for a cure for a liver infection.

The Shaftesbury association also got Locke implicated in the Rye House Plot – a scheme to assassinate Charles II and his Catholic brother who was also heir to the throne.

Despite the liberal politics of his published work, Locke was a investor in the Royal Africa Company, which was founded by royal charter in 1672 for the sale of slaves to the plantations.

The *Wealth of Nations*

Like many of his contemporaries, Locke identified wealth with money – and specifically with reserves of gold. For Locke, consumable goods were all too easily used up and too unreliable, whereas money was hard to use up and consume and was therefore what wealth really consisted in.

From this it followed that the goal of a nation's political economy should be to hoard things like gold (at the time, money was made from precious metals). This idea found its most famous critic in a Scotsman, **Adam Smith** (1723–90), and his book, the *Wealth of Nations* (1776).

THE MOST OBVIOUS THING WRONG WITH LOCKE'S IDEA IS THAT HE COMPLETELY MISUNDERSTOOD WHAT MAKES COUNTRIES WEALTHY.

Smith believed that the best way to promote trade was to trust to the self-interest and inventiveness of individual traders.

"It is not from the benevolence of the butcher, the brewer, or the baker, that we expect our dinner, but from their regard to their own interest. We address ourselves, not to their humanity but to their self-love, and never talk to them of our own necessities but of their advantages."

Wealth of Nations, Book 1, Chapter 2

Self-interest

IT IS SELF-INTEREST THAT LEADS WORKERS TO DO WHAT IS BEST FOR SOCIETY IN GENERAL.

THINK OF IT LIKE THIS: IF FOOD IS SCARCE, PRICES WILL GO UP; IF PRICES GO UP, THERE WILL BE MORE MONEY TO BE MADE BY MAKING OR IMPORTING FOOD.

AS A RESULT, MORE PEOPLE WILL START SUPPLYING FOOD, WITH THE RESULT THAT FOOD WILL BECOME PLENTIFUL AGAIN AND PRICES WILL NORMALISE.

Similarly, if a company produces shoddy goods, people will buy from other places; so it is in the company's interest to make good-quality products. The self-correcting nature of the market led Smith to think that we could trust the market to provide what was needed – and the principal obstacle to the market trading freely and fulfilling our needs was government intervention.

The Invisible Hand

Without government intervention, Smith believed that the market would run smoothly and people's self-interest would lead to them benefiting those around them as though their behaviour were guided by an "invisible hand".

In practice, the invisible hand works some of the time. While there are companies that continue to stay in business selling badly-made products, the majority of goods are reasonably well made and are plentifully available, at least in the developed world.

HOWEVER, THERE ARE THINGS, LIKE ROADS, THAT ARE BETTER PROVIDED BY GOVERNMENTS THAN BY THE MARKET.

For Smith, there are definitely things that governments should do:

First the duty of protecting the society from the violence and invasion of other independent societies; secondly the duty of protecting as far as possible, every member of the society from the injustice or oppression of every other member of it and thirdly the duty of erecting and maintaining public works and certain public institutions.

Wealth of Nations,
Book 4, Chapter 9

The invisible hand follows profit, and works less well at providing for needs where the route to making money is less obvious. Aware of this limitation, Smith believed that the state should pay for things like public education to stop people from becoming too stupid.

40

While the value of goods depends on their scarcity, Smith went further, saying that the value of a thing consists in the amount of labour one could get in exchange for it. Labour was the key ingredient in the cost of production of a thing, which determined its value, or at least the minimum price that would make its production profitable.

The real price of every thing, what every thing really costs to the man who wants to acquire it, is the toil and trouble of acquiring it. What every thing is really worth to the man who has acquired it and who wants to dispose of it, or exchange it for something else, is the toil and trouble which it can save to himself, and which it can impose upon other people. What is bought with money, or with goods, is purchased by labour.

Wealth of Nations, Book 1, Chapter 5

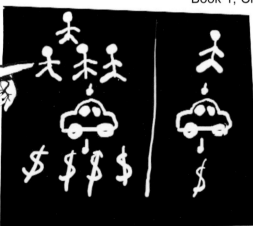

This idea became known as the Labour Theory of Value, and was the bedrock of "classical" economics. It led Smith to agree with Hobbes' phrase "wealth is power" – not because wealth automatically gives its owner political power, but because it gives him or her control of other people's labour.

Specialization of Skills

Smith believed that economic growth stems from specialization. The best way to maximize profit and the efficiency of production was for people to specialize in a few select skills, rather than produce whole products themselves.

Smith thought that specialization and efficiency of production was the very mark of progress. Humanity moved from societies where people lived in small, self-sufficient units to larger societies where workers each possessed a single skill.

A whole country could conceivably be centred around a single industry, like the oil empires of the Middle East, getting almost everything it needs via trade. Smith proved to be spot-on, and the sort of specialization he described has been widely adopted.

Free Trade

As a believer in free trade, Smith was opposed to the tariffs and restrictions that Britain was putting on many of the colonies of its burgeoning empire. The American colonists, for example, were barely allowed to manufacture anything for themselves, and goods that they needed from other parts of the empire (e.g. tea) all had to pass through London, where they were subject to additional tariffs.

IN THE LONG RUN, THESE TARIFFS STIFLE TRADE, WHILE THEIR PURPOSE IS TO MAKE THE HOME NATION RICHER.

MOREOVER, THE STRICT CONTROL THAT EUROPEAN NATIONS EXERT OVER THEIR COLONIES IS A GREAT DRAIN ON RESOURCES.

I HAD BEEN THINKING ABOUT THIS FOR SOME TIME BEFORE THE WEALTH OF NATIONS WAS PUBLISHED IN 1776 – ONE YEAR AFTER THE AMERICAN REVOLUTION BEGAN.

Not that the British government learned its lesson – it was still imposing a salt monopoly in India in the 20th century.

The Scottish Enlightenment

Smith spent most of his life in Edinburgh, and was one of the shining lights of the Scottish Enlightenment. He counted the philosopher David Hume as a personal friend. Riding on the back of the new wealth that was pouring into Edinburgh after unification with England, the men of the Enlightenment set about waking Scotland from her dogmatic slumbers.

Smith is generally considered to be the father of modern economics, though the *Wealth of Nations* is not wholly original.

PARTS OF IT COME FROM A FRENCH GROUP CALLED THE PHYSIOCRATS, AND MUCH OF IT HAD BEEN PRE-EMPTED BY **ANDERS CHYDENIUS** (1729–1803), A SWEDISH PRIEST, IN A BOOK CALLED *THE NATIONAL GAIN* THAT WAS PUBLISHED ELEVEN YEARS PREVIOUSLY.

David Hume
(1711– 76)

But it was to Smith that most subsequent economists looked.

The Slave Trade

WHEN I BEGAN THE *WEALTH OF NATIONS* I WAS BETTER KNOWN AS A MORAL PHILOSOPHER, AND MY WORK SHOULDN'T BE SEEN AS TOO FAR REMOVED FROM MY MORAL PHILOSOPHY.

IN SOME RESPECTS THE BOOK MIGHT HAVE BEEN BETTER TITLED THE *WELFARE OF NATIONS*.

By the time Smith died in 1790, the British were dominating international trade and the Industrial Revolution had just kicked off in Britain (although historians disagree about the exact date).

However, the British colonies in the West Indies and North America that had helped bankroll this development relied heavily on slave labour to run their sugar and cotton plantations. It is now believed that around 20 million people were taken from their homes in Africa to work as slaves on plantations in British colonies and in the newly independent USA. Over half died on the journey.

The Rothschilds

Meanwhile, in the Jewish ghetto of Frankfurt-am-Main, **Mayer Rothschild** (1744–1812) and his sons had begun building the now famous finance house. What made their business unique was that Rothschild sent his five sons to open branches in the five busiest cities in Europe.

The Rothschilds developed the very idea of the international investment bank – they could transfer their funds wherever there was peace and prosperity, and thus enjoy high interest on their investments no matter what the situation was. Importantly, they were happy to fund private and government ventures by lending money. These two factors made them a financial machine of a completely new sort.

During the Napoleonic wars (1799–1815) the family made the vast fortunes for which they are famous to this day. The Rothschilds eventually opted to side with the British, which was probably one significant factor in deciding the outcome of the war. They helped finance Britain's heavy subsidies to its allies by lending money to the government, and used their private trafficking network to provide money to the Duke of Wellington during his Spanish campaign.

IT IS OFTEN SAID THAT WHEN NAPOLEON WAS FINALLY DEFEATED IN WATERLOO, MY SON NATHAN, OUR REPRESENTATIVE IN LONDON, GOT TO HEAR OF IT FIRST VIA OUR PRIVATE NETWORK.

WHILE EVERYBODY IN LONDON WAS SELLING FRANTICALLY, FRIGHTENED BY NAPOLEON'S RETURN, HE CAME IN AND BOUGHT EVERYTHING AT VERY LOW PRICES.

The Rothschilds anticipated by a few decades the appearance of the self-made tycoons owning a fortune that only national treasuries could accumulate until then.

Industrialization

In the early 19th century, the Industrial Revolution was really hotting up in Britain. Its development relied heavily on the improvements made to the steam engine made by **James Watt** (1763–1819).

The public flocked to gaze at these wonders of the new world in the Great Exhibition of 1851.

Industrialization finally drove the West out of a mercantile economy and into a capitalist one. Before industrialization, the most important factor in determining the wealth of a country was its **volume** of trade, or exports minus imports. After industrialization, the **value** of what a country could produce became more important.

Industry could now exploit raw materials at a pace far beyond the ability of the colonies to provide them. To have available raw materials cheaply and in abundance, the colonies themselves had to be mechanized.

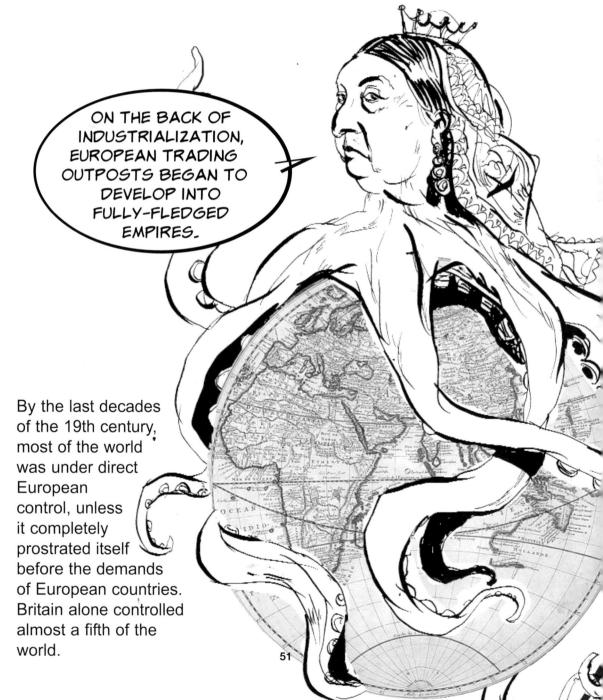

ON THE BACK OF INDUSTRIALIZATION, EUROPEAN TRADING OUTPOSTS BEGAN TO DEVELOP INTO FULLY-FLEDGED EMPIRES.

By the last decades of the 19th century, most of the world was under direct European control, unless it completely prostrated itself before the demands of European countries. Britain alone controlled almost a fifth of the world.

The Opium Wars

The European empires were not averse to using force to further their own economic interests. The British East India Company even had its own private army.

In the late 1830s, China stepped up its efforts to stop the trade in opium and this led to the Opium Wars of 1839–42 and 1856–60.

At the end of the second Opium War (in which it was joined by France), Britain forced the Chinese to fully legalize both the trade in opium and the shipment of Chinese indentured labourers to the Americas (where they worked as slaves in all but name).

The Rise of Social Sciences

The boom in industry also meant that science was finally getting the respect it was looking for from all angles of society.

EVEN HARDENED CONSERVATIVES, RELUCTANT TO ADMIT SOMETHING LIKE EVOLUTION, HAD TO RESPECT PHYSICS, ENGINEERING AND CHEMISTRY ONCE THEY BECAME A SOURCE FOR POWER AND WEALTH.

Going along with this increased respect for natural science, preliminary attempts were made to analyse human society and social interaction by scientific means. Sociology, psychology and economics began to look more and more like scientific disciplines.

Smith's *Wealth of Nations* formed the backbone of this new science of economics, but his definitions, concepts and claims were phrased more rigorously, formulated mathematically, and supplemented by empirical data analysed statistically.

David Ricardo

The most influential of the first scientific formulations of what came to be known as "classical" economics was made by **David Ricardo** (1772–1823), in his *Principles of Political Economy and Taxation*, published in 1817.

Ricardo accepted Smith's Labour Theory of Value as a guiding principle governing the major economic variables like costs, profits, prices, employment and wages.

THE REAL MARKET PRICE OF ANY PRODUCT WILL TEND TO FLUCTUATE AROUND THE COST OF THE LABOUR NEEDED TO PRODUCE IT, BECAUSE OF CHANGES IN THE SUPPLY AND DEMAND OF LABOUR – THE AMOUNT OF AVAILABLE JOBS VS. THE NUMBER OF WORKERS WAITING TO FILL THEM.

The Cost of Labour

Since the cost of labour determines all major economic factors, how much of anything is being bought or sold has no significant economic consequences, in Ricardo's view. It follows that the volume of trade does not affect the economic situation, which supports Smith's belief that ultimately government interference with free trade has no beneficial economic effects.

THERE ARE THREE MAIN PLAYERS INVOLVED IN PRODUCTION: THE CAPITALISTS, THE WORKERS AND THE LANDOWNERS.

For Ricardo, differences in rent charged by landowners are due to differences in the productivity of different regions – whether we're talking about more fertile grounds for agriculture, or regions rich in vital industrial resources like coal.

So the more productive a region becomes, the higher the rent will get and the wealthier the landowners. On the other hand, the more productive a region gets, the more capital it produces, so the capitalists will get richer too.

THIS IS THE BASIC REASONING BEHIND TWO OF MY MOST FAMOUS ASSERTIONS.

THE FIRST STATES THAT THE MORE PRODUCTIVE YOU ARE, THE WEALTHIER YOU GET. THIS IS THE BEDROCK OF "CLASSICAL" ECONOMICS AND CAPITALIST IDEOLOGY.

However, it will become clear that this simple faith in productivity is far too optimistic.

The Workers' Straitjacket

Ricardo's second principle is that labour is destined never to become more expensive. From the Labour Theory of Value it follows that all increases in productivity and profit principally happen because labour got cheaper.

This means that workers can expect to get more money as society becomes more advanced, but only because more money is produced. As more of it is produced, it skews the balance of supply vs. demand and so causes inflation – it is as if money itself gets cheaper. So the rate at which wages increase will tend to be the same as the rate of inflation – nominal but never real, in economic terms.

THIS LEAVES THE WORKING CLASS IN A STRAITJACKET, FOR NO MATTER HOW MUCH THEY PRODUCE, THEIR CONDITIONS OF LIVING WILL NEVER GET ANY BETTER.

John Stuart Mill

This grim result for the workers was presented by Ricardo as a problem to be dealt with. But Ricardo never doubted that industrialization and progress were the only way to create a stronger and richer society. The best that workers can hope for is a condition of full employment, and that can be achieved only by increasing production at a rate matching the growth of the population. This solution, however, was not enough for the most prominent thinker of classical liberal ideology – **John Stuart Mill** (1806–73).

RICARDO WAS A FREQUENT VISITOR TO OUR HOUSEHOLD WHEN I WAS GROWING UP, AS HE WAS IN CLOSE CONTACT WITH THE UTILITARIAN SCHOOL OF THINKERS, WHOSE CHIEF MEMBERS WERE **JEREMY BENTHAM (1748–1832)** AND MY FATHER **JAMES MILL (1773–1836)**.

MY AIM IN ECONOMICS WAS ALWAYS TO COMBINE UTILITARIANISM WITH RICARDIAN ECONOMICS.

Utilitarianism

Jeremy Bentham

> UTILITARIANISM IS BASED ON THE PRINCIPLE OF THE GREATEST HAPPINESS FOR THE GREATEST NUMBER, WHICH I CALL THE PRINCIPLE OF UTILITY.

> THE MORALLY AND POLITICALLY RIGHT THING TO DO, ACCORDING TO THIS PRINCIPLE, IS THE ONE THAT MAXIMIZES PLEASURE OR MINIMIZES PAIN TO THE GREATEST DEGREE FOR THE GREATEST NUMBER OF PEOPLE.

Utilitarianism was designed to be an empirical, scientific "calculus" for solving ethical and political problems. It was meant to provide a new ground for liberal thought, as the old Lockean "natural rights" and "social contract" now sounded too abstract, unscientific and outdated. Utilitarianism gradually became the dominant world view of modern liberal politics and capitalist economics.

The Pleasures of Freedom

This was the basis behind Bentham's liberal politics, which aimed to minimize state intervention in private affairs, including the economy. Bentham and his school were considered part of the "radical" movement. One central "radical" idea they had was that everyone should have the vote, including women and the poor, an idea for which Bentham was scornfully booed out of Parliament. He also thought that homosexuality should be legalized and same-sex marriages be allowed, but he never published these opinions for fear of the response.

Rules of Nature and Society

Mill saw the state and the market as instruments designed to serve the individual, and ultimately to increase the happiness of all. This involved not only maximizing prosperity but giving people the freedom to form their own opinions and live by them.

I DISTINGUISHED BETWEEN TWO KINDS OF RULES: RULES OF **NATURE** AND RULES OF **SOCIETY**. THE LATTER ARE PRODUCTS OF HUMAN DECISION AND SHOULD BE MADE WITH A VIEW TO THE ESSENTIAL FREEDOM OF EVERY INDIVIDUAL.

In Ricardian economics, rules of nature govern production. There are natural, physical limitations on how much we can produce – whatever we do, there is a finite amount of land suitable for farming, a finite number of fish in the sea, etc. But distribution is governed by social rules, deciding who gets to enjoy the commodities and wealth produced. It is here that the state should come in as a regulating factor.

Distribution of Wealth

The main economic instrument of the state is taxation. Deciding who, what and how much to tax could be a decisive factor in the way wealth is distributed throughout the population. Mill thought that taxation should be the means to publicly fund education, health, legal aid and basic living conditions for all citizens. To this day, this is a landmark of liberal economics and politics.

> BUT TO BELIEVE THAT THE CONDITION OF WORKERS CAN SIGNIFICANTLY IMPROVE THROUGH PROGRESS, I HAD TO POINT OUT WHERE THE FAULT IN RICARDO'S REASONING LAY.

> AS A RESULT, DESPITE SETTING OUT SIMPLY TO ADAPT RICARDO'S THEORIES, I ENDED UP CHANGING THE FACE OF ECONOMICS ...

Supply and Demand

It is not enough to produce the commodity; you need to get it to the customers, let them know about it, compete with other available brands and so on. So it is not only labour that determines the price of goods, but also the costs involved in selling them.

Mill paved the way beyond the Labour Theory of Value and towards the Supply and Demand theory that replaced it, and which is still prevalent in economic theory today. This theory received its first detailed analysis in **Alfred Marshall**'s (1842–1924) *Principles of Economics* of 1881.

The equilibrium point rotates around: consumer spend = cost + profit.

For Mill, we find that a variety of factors determine that equilibrium point between buyers and sellers. These factors include, but are not limited to, labour. This means that not all the profit made from an item is what it makes above the cost of labour.

Mill thought that this increase must come initially in the form of education, health, hygiene and public transport. Better educated and cleaner workers could be trusted to spend their money in worthwhile ways. He also supported public assistance for women who wanted to get a career.

Humane Capitalism?

Mill's was the first liberal theory to respond to the results of the Industrial Revolution.

I PICTURED A STATE WHICH COMBINES PUBLIC SPENDING TO ALLOW PEOPLE TO DEVELOP THEMSELVES MORE COMPLETELY (INCLUDING BASIC HEALTH, EDUCATION, WORKING CONDITIONS, ETC.) WITH THE IDEA THAT PRIVATE ENTERPRISE SERVES THE GREATER GOOD.

These ideas form one side of the broad church of "liberalism" – both sides broadly agree about the state staying out of private affairs, but they disagree about how the state should put this into effect economically.

On the other side, more right-wing thinkers put emphasis on the state staying out of economic affairs, because they believe this hands-off approach best serves development.

Mill continued the Utilitarian tradition, presenting a humane form of capitalism and supporting private interest because it was supposed to benefit the general good – even though industrialization made living conditions a lot worse for the great majority of the population.

Without any legal limit on working hours or minimum wages, the working day lasted for sixteen hours and the pay sufficed for only the most meagre existence. Trade unions began to form, but they could do little as long as labour was unskilled and each worker immediately replaceable by another.

BEFORE INDUSTRY, MOST OF THE POPULATION LIVED IN THE COUNTRYSIDE AND WORKED IN AGRICULTURE.

AFTER INDUSTRIALIZATION, FOOD PRODUCTION BECAME MUCH EASIER, AND A NEW DEMAND FOR WORKING HANDS WAS CREATED IN THE CITIES, WHICH RAPIDLY EXPANDED AND GREW EXTREMELY OVERCROWDED.

None grew bigger or more crowded than London. During the 19th century, most workers were crammed into little rooms in slum areas that stretched all over the city.

Charles Dickens (1812–70)

Life in the Slums

Many of the slums were built below the level of the Thames at high tide, which meant they became a natural toilet bowl that flushed twice daily. A cholera epidemic unsurprisingly hit London in 1841. But only after the "Great Stink" of 1858 threatened to bring Parliament to a close did the building of a sewerage system begin in earnest. Meanwhile, the air was being increasingly polluted by coal-burning factories, producing the notorious smog that covered the city.

MORTALITY RATES AMONG CHILDREN OF THE WORKING CLASS REACHED 80 PER CENT.

LIFE EXPECTANCY WAS SUCH THAT MANY OF US WHO DID SURVIVE BECAME ORPHANS.

ORPHANAGES FUNDED BY PHILANTHROPISTS, AND THE HOSPITAL FOR SICK CHILDREN, OPENED IN 1852, COULD IMPROVE THINGS ONLY A LITTLE.

The wretchedness of the working class was depicted in the works of Charles Dickens, Victor Hugo and others.

The Great Famine

Conditions were similar throughout the industrializing world. In Ireland, the Great Famine of 1845–50 was exacerbated by the British government's insistence on a hands-off approach to managing the economy, with the result that, despite horrendous conditions, Ireland was a net exporter of food during the years of the great hunger. The population reduced by 20–25 per cent – almost 1 in 4 either died or emigrated.

Movements for Reform

Mill found that his liberal response to these conditions convinced only a minority in Parliament, which prior to the Reform Act of 1867 represented mainly the gentry and the rich. With the government all but deaf to the pleas of the majority of the population, reform and protest movements sprung up outside Parliament. The first of these was led by **Robert Owen** (1771–1858), a self-made man who earned his fortune in the textile industry.

IN 1799 I BOUGHT A CHAIN OF MILLS CALLED "NEW LANARK" NEAR GLASGOW. THE SELLER HAD CREATED A SMALL VILLAGE FOR HIS WORKERS, INCLUDING CHILDCARE, A HEALTH SERVICE, ETC.

HE WOULD SELL ONLY ON CONDITION THAT HIS WORKERS WOULD CONTINUE TO RECEIVE THE SAME TREATMENT.

Owen took his promise seriously, and even improved on his workers' conditions, especially in setting up a school for the children, which meant removing them from the workforce.

GRADUALLY I CAME TO CONCEIVE NEW LANARK AS A MODEL FOR HOW ALL INDUSTRY SHOULD BE – WITH COMMUNITIES OF WORKERS LIVING AROUND THE MAIN FACTORIES, RECEIVING ALL THEIR NEEDS AS PART OF THEIR WORKING CONDITIONS.

Owen is sometimes considered a founder of socialism, but what he was offering was really a kind of conscientious capitalism, and he never supported giving political power to the working class. For a while he sparked the interest of the growing trade unions, but his worker colonies soon collapsed after his death.

The Chartists

Nevertheless, Owen's ideas did have a lasting effect, feeding into perhaps the greatest reform movement in Britain until the Suffragettes – the loose coalition known as The Chartists. The Chartists were made up of the new industrial working class, artisans and some middle-class professionals. They had many – sometimes conflicting – interests, but they united in support of the "People's Charter" that was drafted by a radical MP called **William Lovett** (1800–77).

I DRAFTED THE CHARTER FROM WHICH WE GOT OUR NAME IN 1838. IT CALLED FOR UNIVERSAL FRANCHISE (THE RIGHT TO VOTE AND BE ELECTED FOR PARLIAMENT) FOR EVERY MAN OVER 21, A SALARY FOR MPS, AN ANNUAL ELECTION, AND A SECRET BALLOT.

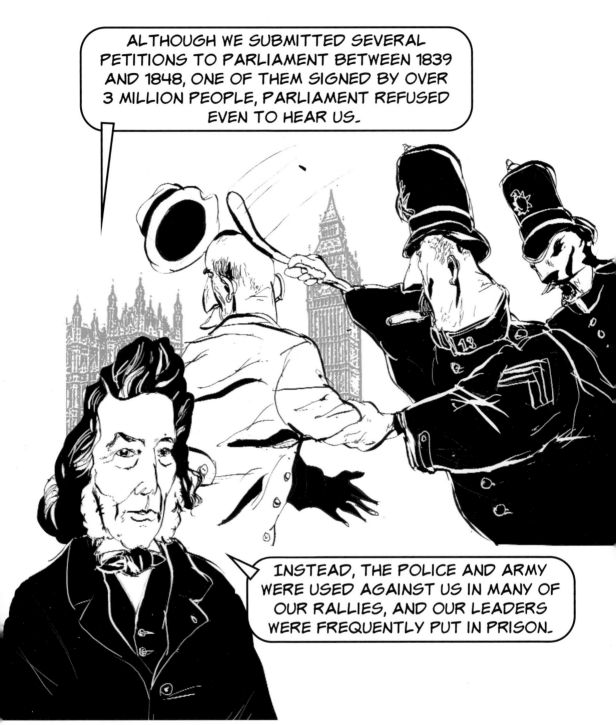

After its third petition was ignored by Parliament in 1848, the movement quickly deteriorated. But its cause was kept alive by a growing number of MPs, especially after the Liberal Party was officially formed in 1859. To avoid losing power completely, it was the Conservatives who eventually accepted almost all the Chartists' demands in the Reform Act of 1867.

The Birth of Socialism

However, by the time of the Reform Act, a bigger challenge to capitalism had evolved in Europe – socialism. Socialism is basically a call for greater equality in political power and the distribution of goods. It managed to rally much of the working class behind it.

The two most influential thinkers in early socialism are probably **Claude-Henri de Saint-Simon** (1760–1825) and **Mikhail Bakunin** (1814–76). Saint-Simon, like many other socialist leaders, was a member of an aristocratic family. But he was a staunch supporter of revolutionary ideas.

MY PRIMARY INTEREST WAS TO BRING ABOUT A NEW AND RATIONAL REORGANIZATION OF SOCIETY.

I CAME UP WITH A VISION OF AN INTERNATIONAL FEDERATION, RUN BY EFFICIENT CLERKS AND EXPERTS TO THE BENEFIT OF SOCIETY, INDUSTRY AND WELFARE.

Saint-Simon himself was hardly a socialist, though he did support a kind of meritocracy.

INDUSTRIES WILL BE RUN BY EXPERTS, NOT BY UNQUALIFIED RICH PEOPLE.

SCIENTISTS WILL REPLACE PRIESTS AND THEOLOGIANS AND BE RESPONSIBLE FOR THE MORAL BACKBONE OF A SOCIETY DEVOTED TO EFFICIENCY, EXPERTISE AND INDUSTRIOUSNESS.

It was really his ability to gather some of the great minds of his day around him that has made Saint-Simon famous. His students turned the school of Saint-Simonism into the leading socialist movement in France.

Control of the Means of Production

IN ADDITION TO MY BELIEF IN A MERITOCRACY, IN WHICH SOCIAL POSITION AND WEALTH WILL DEPEND SOLELY ON SKILL, TALENT AND LEARNING, SAINT-SIMONISTS STAND FOR THE ABOLITION OF PRIVATE PROPERTY AND THE MODERN STATE THAT THEY SEE EVOLVING AROUND THEM.

Saint-Simonism highlights one significant aspect of socialism – the social control of the means of production. Socialism calls for what it considers a more rational way of distribution – taking into account the general benefit and not the personal interest of any single party. This is diametrically opposed to the liberal capitalist view that private ownership results in the most rational market.

Bakunin and Anarchism

Bakunin, on the other hand, represents the more revolutionary concerns of socialism, and its mistrust of states and control altogether. He believed that states and government are simply means of exploiting the working class. As such, the workers should not seek political power. Rather, they should aim for the abolition of the state, as its continued existence can be used only to subjugate them to the ruling class. This makes Bakunin one of the fathers of anarchism as much as socialism.

THE WORKERS MUST FORM A REVOLUTIONARY FORCE AIMING TO ABOLISH ALL STATE POWER COMPLETELY.

NO ONE SHOULD BE CONSIDERED THE OWNER OF THE MEANS OF PRODUCTION, AND THE DIFFERENCE BETWEEN WORK AND LEISURE SHOULD BE ERASED.

THE MEANS OF PRODUCTION SHOULD BE OPEN TO ALL, USED TO PRODUCE WHATEVER THEY WISH, AND THOUGHT OF AS NO DIFFERENT FROM RECREATIONAL PARKS.

Marx, the anti-Utopian

However, these thinkers and other early socialists were all surpassed by the work of **Karl Marx** (1818–83), the thinker whose name became almost synonymous with extreme socialism.

I CALLED ALL THE SOCIALISTS BEFORE ME "UTOPIAN SOCIALISTS". THEY IMAGINED A JUST SOCIETY, AND CALLED UPON PEOPLE TO MAKE IT REAL.

THEIR THOUGHT WAS NOT BASED ON A THEORY OF SOCIETY AND THE RULES THAT GOVERN IT, AND THEY HAD NO IDEA WHAT PROCESSES WOULD BRING THEIR SOCIETY ABOUT.

Moreover, said Marx, they had no idea how capitalism worked, how it came about, and what it must lead to. They still thought within the outdated framework of the social contract thinkers like Hobbes and Locke, imagining that people can just design a society as they see fit.

Marx and Hegel

Marx, on the other hand, in his mature thought presented a complete theory of society and economics, and the historical forces that shape them. He had a deep understanding of economic theory, and he could account for how the very structures of capitalism would inevitably lead to its collapse. He presented his view as "Scientific Socialism", a socialism that follows as a scientific conclusion.

The theoretical framework he used for this purpose relied heavily on the philosophy of **Georg Wilhelm Friedrich Hegel** (1770–1831).

THE MAIN INGREDIENT MISSING FROM THE THOUGHT OF THE 18TH-CENTURY ENLIGHTENMENT WAS A PROPER UNDERSTANDING OF HISTORY.

Resolving the Contradictions

Hegelian history proceeds according to rules of its own. Specifically, history moves forward as the contradictions between ideologies are resolved. For Hegel, this evolutionary path is predetermined and does not depend on people's choices.

Thesis–Antithesis–Synthesis

For example, consider the ideas of the general good vs. personal freedom. These are opposing ideas, each represented in history, for instance, in the opposition between Hobbes' "Leviathan" and Locke's natural right to freedom. Eventually, the historical struggle between these two ideas will lead to a resolution.

HEGEL'S APPROACH IS DIALECTICAL.

THIS MEANS THAT THE BASIC ELEMENTS IN HIS SYSTEM ARE TWO OPPOSING IDEAS, CALLED THE **THESIS** AND THE **ANTITHESIS**. THE HISTORICAL STRUGGLE BETWEEN THEM WILL INEVITABLY LEAD TO A RESOLUTION OR **SYNTHESIS** OF BOTH.

This synthesis will then become a new thesis which will stand opposed to a new antithesis, and the process of historical development will continue.

The End of History?

Eventually there will come an "end of history", in which all contradictions dissolve into the highest synthesis. This highest synthesis will have no antithesis and so the historical process will come to an end.

HEGEL THOUGHT THAT SYNTHESIS WAS PROVIDED BY HIS THEORY OF THE RESOLUTION OF THE CONFLICT BETWEEN STATE AND CIVIL SOCIETY.

THE STATE WILL BE RESPONSIBLE FOR COMMON VALUES AND NATIONAL IDENTITY, AND CIVIL SOCIETY WILL BE RESPONSIBLE FOR ECONOMIC NEEDS.

In general, Hegel viewed his own theory as the highest synthesis. Specifically, he thought that history ended with the battle of Jena in 1806, and that the Prussian state of his day was the final realization of reason and the fully realized state. Many have found it hard to agree with this claim, but nevertheless, the general framework of his thought has been widely adopted.

Historical Materialism

Marx claimed to have "inverted" Hegel's theory. Instead of Hegel's **Historical Idealism**, Marx created **Historical Materialism**. Like Hegel, he thought that history is driven forward by an internal dialectic and that contradictions are its driving force. But for Marx that dialectic is not the product of reason or *ideology*, but rather of the *material* satisfaction of needs.

PEOPLE ARE NOT PRIMARILY DIVIDED OVER ABSTRACT ISSUES LIKE PERSONAL FREEDOM OR THE GENERAL GOOD.

WHAT CONCERNS PEOPLE FIRST AND FOREMOST IS HOW TO MAINTAIN OR INCREASE THEIR MATERIAL STANDARD OF LIVING.

So the main struggles and social contradictions do not occur between ideological parties, but rather between classes – social groups that have a common relation to the means of production of goods.

The History of Class Struggles

For Marx, the different aspects of culture and civilization are products of a particular class structure, and are designed to support, justify and protect that structure. So society is constructed around one particular dominant class – the class that owns the principal means of production of an age. This is what lies behind the statement in the *Communist Manifesto* (1848):

To take an example, ancient Greece and Rome ran on a slave economy. Slaves were the principal means of production, and slave-owners the ruling class. According to Marx, their culture – politics, ethics, art, philosophy – reflected that fact.

For example, they considered citizenship to be a natural trait of mankind. People not of their citizenship were thus considered essentially of a different nature. Those not sharing their politics and culture were not even considered fully human, and so there was nothing wrong in enslaving them.

AS THE MEANS OF PRODUCTION IMPROVE, THERE GRADUALLY COMES A SHIFT IN POWER. THIS SHIFT CAUSES INCREASING QUANTITIES OF POWER TO GO TO SOME SUBORDINATE CLASS.

IT GROWS STRONGER UNTIL IT GAINS ENOUGH POWER TO OVERTHROW THE REGIME THAT CONTROLS IT, AND WITH IT THE ENTIRE CIVILIZATION IS EITHER DESTROYED OR REVOLUTIONIZED.

This is how the bourgeoisie, the factory-owners and traders, grew stronger as a result of the new trade frontiers in America, Africa and the Far East. Eventually they brought down the feudal world, and created the modern capitalist world in their image.

FREE TRADE, NATURAL RIGHTS, AND THE PICTURE OF PEOPLE AS COMPETING INDIVIDUALS WHO ARE ONLY CONTRACTUALLY OBLIGED TO EACH OTHER – THESE ARE ALL IDEOLOGICAL TOOLS OF CAPITALISM.

Similarly, for Marx, liberal democratic politics is just a means to keep politics helplessly tied to capital. For whenever individuals compete economically with each other under equal terms, the one with the most money is almost sure to win.

Das Kapital

Marx's most mature presentation of his thought comes in his voluminous masterpiece, *Das Kapital* (1867–94), on which he worked from the mid-1850s, and which was completed posthumously by **Friedrich Engels** (1820–95), his close friend and colleague. In this work, Marx abandons philosophy for the sake of economic analysis.

KAPITAL PRESENTS A DETAILED ANALYSIS OF THE WORKINGS OF CAPITALISM, SHOWING THAT IT MUST FIRST SPREAD OUT GLOBALLY AND THEN NECESSARILY BRING ITS OWN DEMISE.

IT IS BASED, LIKE ALL ECONOMIC WORK OF THE TIME, ON THE LABOUR THEORY OF VALUE.

Value = Human Labour

But Marx takes the Labour Theory to an extreme. For liberal economists, the Labour Theory was a guiding principle to analyse fluctuations in the price of a commodity. Marx takes the Labour Theory to mean that all value represents human labour, and so the value of a product is just the amount of human labour needed to produce it.

THE CLASS RESPONSIBLE FOR PRODUCING THE VALUE OF A PRODUCT IS THE WORKING CLASS, WHICH INVESTS ITS LABOUR.

SO, USING THE LABOUR THEORY, THE MARKET VALUE OF THE PRODUCT WILL REPRESENT THE AMOUNT OF WORKERS' LABOUR.

It follows that the only way for the ruling class to make a profit is to take part of that value for themselves.

APPROPRIATING THE VALUE PRODUCED BY ANOTHER'S LABOUR IS WHAT I CALLED "EXPLOITATION".

SO WE CAN SAY THAT ALL PROFIT WHERE THE WORKERS DON'T OWN THE MEANS OF PRODUCTION IS BASED ON EXPLOITATION.

IN THIS SITUATION, NEITHER THE WORKERS NOR THE CAPITALISTS REALLY CARE ABOUT THE PRODUCTS THEY MAKE – THEIR VALUE IS COMPLETELY DISPLACED BY THE MONEY THEY MAKE. AS A RESULT, THE WORKERS BECOME INCREASINGLY REMOVED FROM WHAT THEY DO. I CALLED THIS PHENOMENON "ALIENATION".

The wages that workers actually get in exchange for their labour equals only the amount that allows them to survive so as to keep on being exploited, and to raise children to be exploited in the future. Workers who are more skilled and irreplaceable may gain a higher standard of living perhaps, but only because they are worth a lot more to their employers than unskilled labourers. The vast majority of the value produced is always taken as profit by the ruling class, who own the means of production.

Surplus Value

The goods produced by labour above what is necessary for survival Marx called the "Surplus Value".

SURPLUS VALUE IS EQUIVALENT TO FREE TIME – TIME NOT SPENT PRODUCING THE MEANS OF SURVIVAL, BUT RATHER IN REST, RECREATION, AND THE PRODUCTION OF CULTURE.

In the capitalist era, Surplus Value is turned into capital – that is the whole basis of the system. The working class becomes the proletariat, who sell their labour on the free market.

So capitalists, according to Marx, quite literally rob the proletariat of their freedom, their culture and their essentially human traits, and force them to work endlessly just to acquire the basic means of survival.

This, according to Marx, is the true face of capitalism. In fact, it is a result of the bourgeoisie doing exactly what a class needs to do in order to gain power – completely transform the means of production, and refashion society to create the conditions that keep it in power. The proletariat needs only to learn how it is done from its oppressors.

Marx's Prediction

Contrary to the popular view, Marx did not predict the formation of communist countries, with which he is so closely identified. Rather, he predicted that capitalism would be utterly successful on a number of fronts.

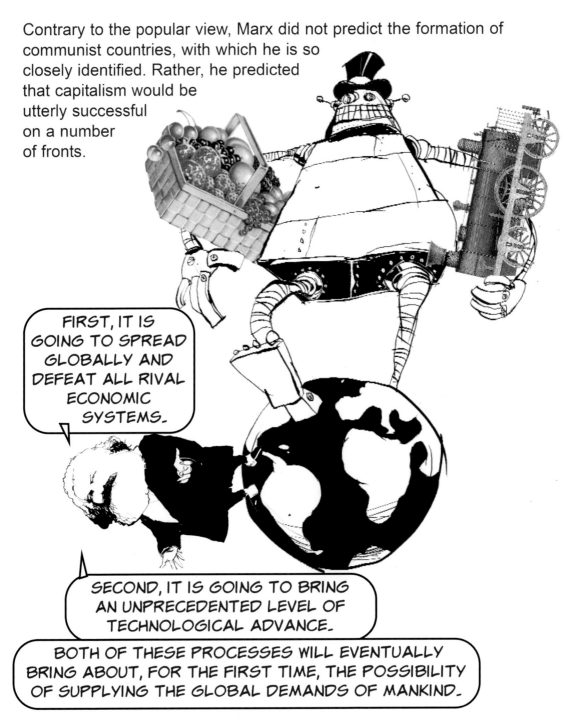

FIRST, IT IS GOING TO SPREAD GLOBALLY AND DEFEAT ALL RIVAL ECONOMIC SYSTEMS.

SECOND, IT IS GOING TO BRING AN UNPRECEDENTED LEVEL OF TECHNOLOGICAL ADVANCE.

BOTH OF THESE PROCESSES WILL EVENTUALLY BRING ABOUT, FOR THE FIRST TIME, THE POSSIBILITY OF SUPPLYING THE GLOBAL DEMANDS OF MANKIND.

Everybody could have everything they wanted, so there would no longer be any real need for class divisions. Capitalism was destined to create the conditions necessary for the coming of the true "end of history", in which all contradictions disappear.

However, for the end of history to come, capitalism must first collapse and make room for true communism. This will necessarily happen, according to Marx, because of the inner workings of capitalism.

CAPITALISM IS DRIVEN TO SEARCH FOR EVER-INCREASING GAIN. UNLIKE FEUDALISM, WHICH COULD MAKE DO WITH A STABLE ECONOMY, CAPITALISM MUST CONSTANTLY GROW.

LAST YEAR'S PROFITS ARE THIS YEAR'S INVESTMENT, AND IT MAKES SENSE TO INVEST CAPITAL ONLY IF YOU HOPE TO GET EVEN MORE CAPITAL OUT OF IT.

There are three ways to increase profit: expand the market, increase the level of exploitation, and improve the technology so as to make production cheaper. As a result, capitalism has to expand across the globe, to improve technologically and to exploit workers to the maximum.

Making a profit will thus become more and more difficult as time goes by, and the economy will tend more and more towards stability. Under these conditions the middle class is destined to disappear, and become part of the proletariat. Capital will be increasingly concentrated in fewer hands of extremely rich capitalists, while the rest will grow increasingly poor.

As this process continues, there will be no escaping the eventual crisis, in which the large majority will no longer be able to support itself. As this happens, the class consciousness of the proletariat will grow, and inevitably the global proletarian revolution will follow.

ESSENTIALLY CAPITALISM, BY ITS VERY SUCCESS, IS CONSTANTLY DIGGING ITS OWN GRAVE.

Capitalism Without Imperialism

Marx thought that capitalism's essential urge to expand and look for further markets and cheaper labour was the driving force behind the European imperialism of the 19th century.

Henry Ford
(1863–1947)

HE THOUGHT THAT THIS BRUTE FORM OF IMPERIALISM WAS PART AND PARCEL OF A CAPITALIST ECONOMY.

BUT THE EXPANSION OF CAPITALISM IN THE 20TH CENTURY WITHOUT TRADITIONAL EMPIRE-BUILDING PROVED HIM WRONG.

But capitalism without some form of imperialism is actually quite a recent development. It was not even seriously considered until the end of the First World War, and not implemented on a global scale until after the Second World War. By then, European countries had lost their world domination to the USA and the Soviet Union.

Imperialism was extracted from capitalism with the arrival in the late 19th century of the big corporations.

BUT THEY DID NOT SO MUCH APPEAR IN THE GREAT EUROPEAN EMPIRES LIKE BRITAIN AND FRANCE.

THEY TENDED TO APPEAR MOSTLY IN THOSE COUNTRIES – LIKE THE USA, GERMANY, AND LATER JAPAN – WHICH HAD TO MAKE DO WITH THE CRUMBS OF THE GLOBAL IMPERIALIST PIE.

Once again, capitalism shows a propensity to develop at the hands of the disadvantaged, those on the lookout for original opportunities for profit (see page 15).

The Rise of the US and Germany

By the time the United States was strong enough to join the imperialist land grab, very few territories remained. Beyond its small island bases in Puerto Rico and Hawaii, the US did little except relieve Spain of its last colonial post in the Philippines, and to force Japan to open itself to foreign trade.

THERE WAS NOTHING LEFT FOR IT TO REACH FOR, BUT THAT DID NOT STOP THE USA FROM HAVING THE FASTEST-GROWING INDUSTRY IN THE WORLD.

GERMANY BECAME A UNIFIED NATION ONLY IN 1871, BUT WAS IMMEDIATELY THE GREATEST INDUSTRIAL POWER IN EUROPE.

Germany made every effort to acquire a small empire in the bits left unclaimed in Africa, China and the Pacific, only to lose it all to Britain after the First World War.

All this was a signal that, by the late 19th century, being the largest empire no longer guaranteed having the largest economy.

> THIS WAS THE TIME OF THE GREAT TYCOONS, PEOPLE WHO TOOK INDUSTRY IN NEW DIRECTIONS AND HELPED TO SHAPE THE CONTEMPORARY WORLD.

> AT&T, DAIMLER-BENZ, COCA-COLA, LEVIS, MITSUBISHI AND OTHER HUGE CORPORATIONS WERE BORN THEN, AS WERE THE OIL EMPIRES OF SHELL AND ROCKEFELLER.

All these corporations owe their international scale of business to Henry Ford's ingenious, widespread use of the production line.

The Production Line

TAKE A LINE OF UNSKILLED WORKERS, TRAINED TO DO A SINGLE JOB LIKE WELD A CAR DOOR ONTO THE MAIN FRAME, PUT THEM AT THE RIGHT SEQUENCE AND YOU GET A CAR.

NOT ONE CAR – HUNDREDS AND EVEN THOUSANDS OF CARS EVERY DAY.

PUT THEM IN DIFFERENT ARRANGEMENTS AND TEACH THEM OTHER SKILLS AND YOU CAN GET ANYTHING FROM BOTTLES OF SOFT DRINKS TO WARSHIPS.

Production capacity rose to levels that not even the early industrialists could dream of. Moreover, it made the cost of each product much lower than previous forms of production, so suddenly the middle classes could afford cars, phones, home electricity and everything else you had to sell.

The "Empires of Trade"

SELLING TO THE MIDDLE CLASSES OPENED UP A HUGE POTENTIAL MARKET, AND SHIFTED THE BALANCE OF TRADE AWAY FROM THE COLONIES AND BACK TO THE WEALTHIER CONSUMERS AT HOME.

In the US, Germany, and later Japan, the new corporate "empires of trade" were founded on the power of the local consumer. The world was gradually turning towards an economy based mainly on trade among the highly industrial nations themselves.

The period up to and beyond the First World War saw unchecked levels of industrialization and development. Marx's idea of the crisis of capitalism seemed the farthest thing from reality, and not even the Bolshevik revolution in Russia and elsewhere could change that.

This growth was particularly felt in the USA, whose involvement in the war was relatively short and far from home. The size of the American army alone rose from about 200,000 men in early 1917 to nearly 4 million, and by the end of the war the US was the strongest country in the world.

The Roaring Twenties

At the end of the war, the economies of the European empires were exhausted. But the American economy kept growing at an unprecedented pace, spurred on by its enhanced industrial capacity and new status as the world's banker. American economic growth was so high that the period came to be known as the "the roaring twenties".

THE TOTAL REALIZED INCOME OF THE USA ROSE BY 20 PER CENT FROM 1923 TO 1929. AT THE SAME TIME PRODUCTIVITY ROSE BY 32 PER CENT.

HOWEVER, MUCH AS MARX PREDICTED, ALL THIS NEW WEALTH CONCENTRATED IN THE HANDS OF A TINY MINORITY.

It was calculated that in 1929, 0.1 per cent of the population controlled 34 per cent of the country's wealth, and owned as much money as the bottom 42 per cent. Corporate profits throughout the 1920s rose by 62 per cent, and the earnings of the top percentage almost doubled, while the average raise for workers was only 9 per cent.

THE CONSERVATIVE COOLIDGE ADMINISTRATION EXACERBATED THE SITUATION BY CUTTING TAXES FOR THE RICH TO A THIRD IN 1926.

AS DID THE SUPREME COURT, WHEN IT RULED THAT THE MINIMUM WAGE LEGISLATION WAS UNCONSTITUTIONAL IN 1923.

With the belief that this rich man's paradise would last forever, speculation in the stock market was sky high, driven forwards by the banks, which were much less regulated than they are today.

The Crash and the Great Depression

But so much money in the hands of so few people meant that industrial supply became much higher than the demand, and profits were declining.

With as few as 200 corporations holding almost half the corporate wealth of the country, the crash quickly led to the collapse of the banking system – the vital life system of a capitalist economy.

The stock market crash hit an already skewed American economy, and this, coupled with some knee-jerk protectionist laws restricting trade, led to the Great Depression. As unemployment rose, its effects were worsened by the lack of any substantial savings or social insurance schemes. Because the European economies were reliant on the USA, the Depression spread across the Atlantic and then all over the globe.

But capitalism was nevertheless extremely shaken, as all over the world economists and politicians tried everything they could in order to bring an end to the Depression, but to no avail.

The New Deal

In the US, the Depression brought an end to a decade of hands-off conservative rule, and the rise of the more interventionist **Franklin D. Roosevelt** (1882–1945). Roosevelt introduced a number of measures to bring the economy back to life using public spending. Collectively, these programmes were called the "New Deal".

THE NEW DEAL WORKED ALONG THREE MAIN FRONTS: THE REGULATION OF THE FINANCE MARKET, THE REGULATION OF THE WORK MARKET, AND THE INCREASE IN PUBLIC WORK.

UNIONS WERE STRENGTHENED AND MINIMUM WAGES AND PENSION SCHEMES WERE IMPOSED.

Billions were invested in public works like laying roads and rail tracks, and restoring natural parks and beaches. And tight controls were placed on banks and the trading of stocks and shares.

Keynes and Liberal Economics

The economic theory behind the New Deal was created by **John Maynard Keynes** (1883–1946), who is known as the "father of modern liberal economics". His ideas set the tone for liberal-democratic economic policy to this day.

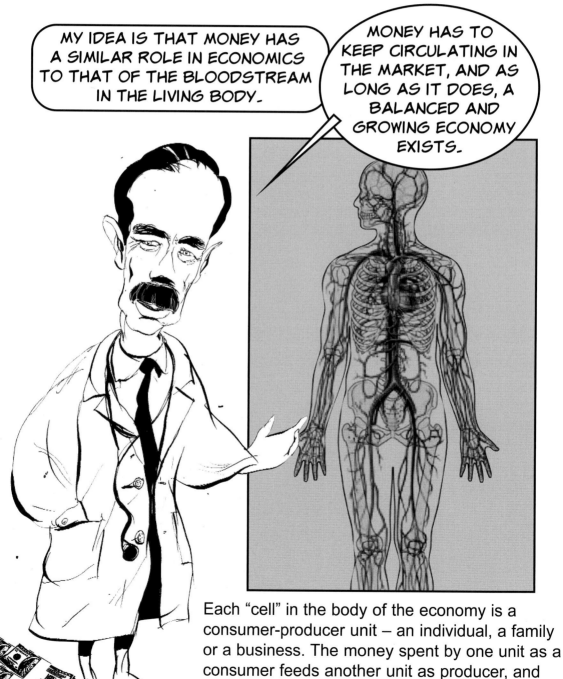

MY IDEA IS THAT MONEY HAS A SIMILAR ROLE IN ECONOMICS TO THAT OF THE BLOODSTREAM IN THE LIVING BODY.

MONEY HAS TO KEEP CIRCULATING IN THE MARKET, AND AS LONG AS IT DOES, A BALANCED AND GROWING ECONOMY EXISTS.

Each "cell" in the body of the economy is a consumer-producer unit – an individual, a family or a business. The money spent by one unit as a consumer feeds another unit as producer, and vice versa.

A Healthy Circulation

Keynes claimed that recessions occur when economic units begin to accumulate money instead of allowing it to circulate. For example, when too much money is accumulated in too few hands, or when investors become wary of the future and decide to start saving money rather than investing it.

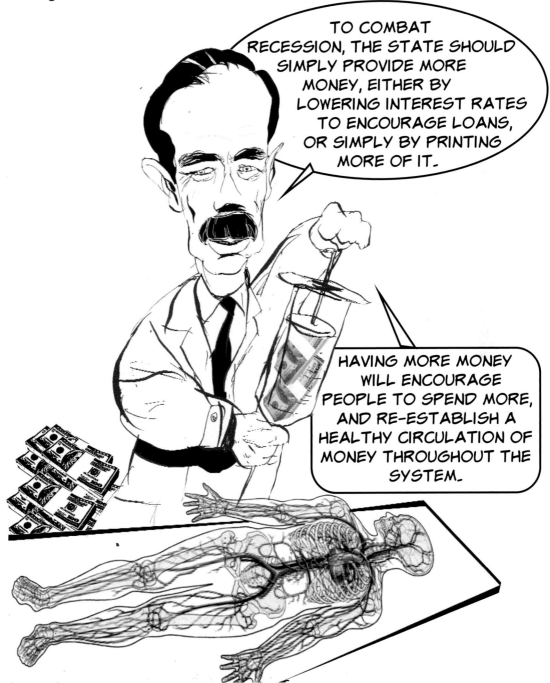

Depressions happen when for some reason (like a stock market crash) the public loses faith in the economy completely, and no amount of money being fed into the market is enough to get it to spend again. In the anatomical analogy, this is similar to a cardiac arrest.

THE ONLY WAY OUT OF A DEPRESSION IS FOR THE STATE TO STEP IN AND DO WHAT THE PUBLIC IS REFUSING TO DO — I.E. SPEND MONEY AND ACT LIKE AN ARTIFICIAL PULSE.

SO THE GOVERNMENT HAS TO COMMISSION PROJECTS, FUND PUBLIC VENTURES, AND ALSO IMPOSE WORKING CONDITIONS AND MINIMUM WAGES THAT FORCE MONEY TO MOVE AGAIN.

The Cycles of Capitalism

Keynes offers the first mature theory of an economy that relies on consumers in the industrialized countries. According to this theory, consumption must remain constantly high for the economy to bloom. As such, it is the backbone of consumer culture.

Keynes claimed that, while unchecked, capitalist markets go through unavoidable cycles of growth and recession. There is no crucial breaking point of the system as Marx thought, but also no possibility of constant growth.

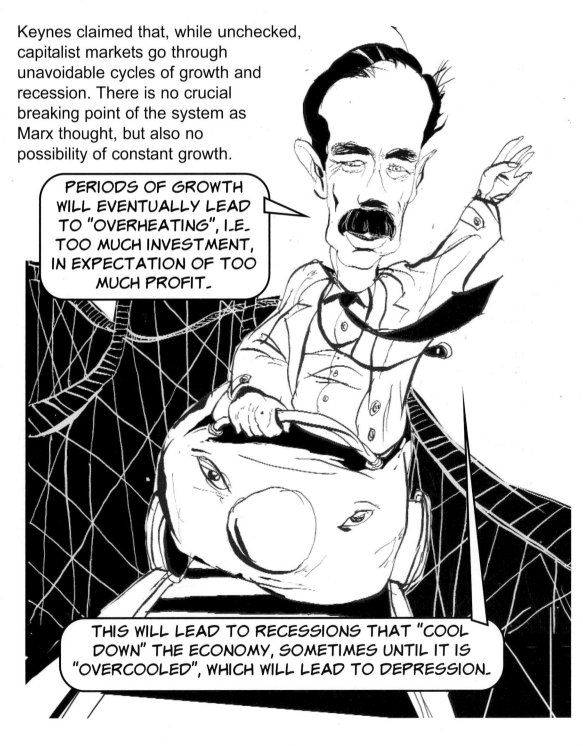

PERIODS OF GROWTH WILL EVENTUALLY LEAD TO "OVERHEATING", I.E. TOO MUCH INVESTMENT, IN EXPECTATION OF TOO MUCH PROFIT.

THIS WILL LEAD TO RECESSIONS THAT "COOL DOWN" THE ECONOMY, SOMETIMES UNTIL IT IS "OVERCOOLED", WHICH WILL LEAD TO DEPRESSION.

Beating Inflation

Inflation is the mark of a heating market, to which the state should respond by reducing the amount of money. This could be done by increasing interest rates, which brings more money into the banks, discourages investors from borrowing and encourages saving.

Fighting Depression

At first, Roosevelt rejected Keynes' ideas, saying he thought his explanation was simply too easy. But eventually only public spending did anything to help the situation, and it increased throughout the 1930s, culminating with the entrance of the US into the Second World War.

DESPITE FAILING TO END THE DEPRESSION, EVEN AFTER THE WAR, RECESSIONS WERE DEALT WITH ACCORDING TO MY GUIDELINES, EVEN BY REPUBLICAN ADMINISTRATIONS, AND NONE TURNED INTO A DEPRESSION.

But whether Keynes' ideas and Roosevelt's policies actually worked is still a matter of opinion. The New Deal probably helped people a bit, but the real recovery from the Great Depression happened only in the 1940s, as a direct result of the Second World War. The Cold War and the spending of the arms race may have helped prevent a depression in the years that followed.

State Capitalism

Meanwhile, in the Far East and many parts of Europe, a different kind of capitalism system was used in order to fight the Great Depression: state-regulated capitalism.

State capitalism is the idea of combining state-funded projects and state regulation of the market with private ownership and profit-making.

STATE CAPITALISM GOES HAND-IN-HAND WITH DICTATORSHIPS, AS THE GOVERNMENT REGULATES MOST ELEMENTS OF PRODUCTION, EMPLOYMENT, WAGES ETC., BUT FACTORIES ARE STILL PRIVATELY OWNED AND ARE GEARED TOWARDS MAXIMUM PROFIT.

This may sound very similar to the economy of the communist bloc, but it commonly rests on an ideology that is diametrically opposed to communism. In effect, in state capitalism a totalitarian government works hand-in-hand with private enterprise.

STATE CAPITALISM CAN IMPOSE REGULATIONS ON LABOUR AND GENERATE A LOT OF IT, ESPECIALLY WHEN WE CAPITALISTS ARE RELUCTANT TO INVEST.

IT COMBINES PRIVATE FINANCIAL GAIN WITH AN OVERVIEW OF THE NEEDS OF THE COUNTRY AS A WHOLE.

IN BAD ECONOMIC CONDITIONS, IT CAN MOTIVATE LOCAL INVESTMENT WHEN OTHER MARKETS LOOK MORE APPEALING TO PRIVATE INVESTORS.

In fact, state capitalism can prove to be a more effective way of developing economies and pulling out of depression than liberal capitalism.

"Economic Miracles"

In China, where the economy was completely devastated in the last days of the empire, the state capitalist initiatives taken between 1928 and 1949 by nationalist leader **Chiang Kai-shek** (1887–1975) helped to put it in relative order (considering he had to fight both Chinese communists and, from 1931, a Japanese invasion).

I STRUGGLED TO REPLACE THE OLD ARISTOCRACY WITH SKILLED PROFESSIONALS AND TO RATIONALIZE THE WAY INDUSTRY WAS RUN.

I ALSO DIRECTED THE WORK INTO PROJECTS THAT BENEFITED THE COUNTRY AS A WHOLE.

Even today, the communist ideology of China masks an increasingly state-capitalistic economic structure, which results in very rapid growth. Moreover, Chiang Kai-shek took his policies to Taiwan in 1949, where they generated an "economic miracle". Similar methods led to similar results in Singapore, South Korea and even Germany before the Second World War.

The Marshall Plan

In the aftermath of the Second World War, much of Europe, China, Korea and Japan lay devastated, and the USA had the only economy capable of reconstructing them, if they were not locked behind the newly-forming "Iron Curtain" of the communist bloc. US **General George Marshall** (1880–1959) drafted the Marshall Plan for the recovery of Europe in 1947.

ON TOP OF EVERYTHING ELSE, THAT WINTER WAS PARTICULARLY HARD, AND THE STATE OF WESTERN EUROPE AND ESPECIALLY GERMANY WAS TURNING INTO A HUMANITARIAN CRISIS.

WHAT'S MORE, THE COMMUNIST COUNTRIES DEALT BETTER WITH THE SITUATION, AT LEAST AT THE LEVEL OF SUPPLYING BASIC FOOD AND SHELTER TO EVERYONE, AND THERE WAS A DANGER OF COMMUNISM ADVANCING WESTWARD.

Loyal to the Keynesian idea of circulation, the Marshall Plan provided $13 billion in aid to Europe, provided the recipients cooperated in an open market. The purpose of the Marshall Plan was two-fold: to get Europe on its feet again and to resist the spread of Soviet Russia.

Of the $13bn, around 90 per cent was a grant that had to be matched by the countries that benefited.

THE MONEY WAS THEN LARGELY SPENT ON AMERICAN GOODS.

THE REMAINING 10 PER CENT WAS A LOAN FROM THE US GOVERNMENT THAT WAS REPAYABLE WITH INTEREST.

BY INVESTING $13BN INDIRECTLY IN ITS OWN ECONOMY, THE US GOVERNMENT CAUSED OVER $26BN TO FLOW BACK TO AMERICA.

In the process, Western Europe recuperated, and got more American money flowing back and forth.

THIS WAS PURE KEYNESIANISM AT WORK. THE COMMUNIST BLOC COULDN'T COMPETE WITH THIS LEVEL OF GROWTH AFTER THE 1960S.

For Europe, however, this meant the end of world domination. The empires that survived the war crumbled within the next twenty years. Europe played second fiddle to either Washington or Moscow for 45 years, and has only recently begun to re-emerge as a world power.

Monetarism vs. Keynesianism

The US administration remained largely committed to Keynesian economics. Even hardened Republicans like Ronald Reagan kept public spending high, though much of it went on foreign aid and military projects like the "Star Wars" programme. Although the US had its fair share of recessions in that period, none of them developed into a depression.

However, Keynesianism is by no means universally accepted. Economists like the American **Milton Friedman** (1912–2006) started questioning the importance of government intervention in the economy, leaving aside cases of extreme depression.

120

The monetarist argument rests on the observation that having more money will change nothing if all prices are adjusted accordingly – if you earn double but everything costs double, you're at exactly the same position. So if the national bank increases the amount of money on the market, businessmen in the long run will adjust their prices so that overall there is no effect on the economy.

BECAUSE BUSINESSMEN NATURALLY ASPIRE TO KEEP EARNING THE SAME REAL AMOUNT WHILE DOING THE LEAST WORK FOR IT, IF MORE MONEY IS PUT INTO THE SYSTEM, THEY WILL INCREASE PRICES ACCORDINGLY.

THIS MEANS THAT IF WE SEE A SHORT-TERM DECREASE IN UNEMPLOYMENT, SAY, BECAUSE OF HAVING MORE MONEY IN THE MARKET, THIS IS JUST BECAUSE THE MARKET HAS NOT ADJUSTED ITSELF YET.

In time, the business community will learn how the national bank responds and adjust itself as appropriate. Some flavour of monetarism has been the prevailing approach from Western central banks since the late 1980s.

One consequence of this theory is that it is unrealistic to expect unemployment to drop below 6 per cent. The national bank should leave it at that and increase the amount of money only at the same rate as the economic growth, more or less.

For Friedman, this is where the response to the Great Depression went wrong. The Federal Reserve failed to intervene, and its inaction resulted in a crisis in banking.

THIS FAILURE TO INTERVENE EFFECTIVELY REDUCED THE AMOUNT OF MONEY IN CIRCULATION, BUT THE SITUATION FOR PEOPLE ON THE GROUND WAS MADE WORSE AS PRICE CONTROL KEPT PRICES ARTIFICIALLY HIGH.

AS A RESULT, THERE WAS LESS MONEY AVAILABLE FOR PEOPLE TO INVEST THEIR WAY OUT OF THE DOWNTURN THAT FOLLOWED THE WALL STREET CRASH, AND WE HAD A DEPRESSION RATHER THAN RECESSION.

Friedman-inspired policies have met with some success at helping troubled economies (e.g. Chile under (the admittedly murderous) General Pinochet).

122

How to Ensure Rising Consumption?

What limits to set on public spending is still one of the major debates in capitalist thinking today, and it forms the rough dividing line between right- and left-wing political thought. However, even Friedman conceded in his later years that he was not quite the monetarist of old.

IN THE END, THE DIFFERENCES BETWEEN MONETARIST AND KEYNESIAN APPROACHES ARE JUST DIFFERENCES IN OPINION ABOUT HOW TO MAXIMIZE STABLE ECONOMIC GROWTH.

BOTH THE DRIVING FORCE AND THE CONSEQUENCE OF THESE ECONOMIC POLICIES IS MORE CONSUMPTION.

Without increasing consumption, the global economy would almost certainly stall.

As consumption has increased in developed countries, so their economies have changed. Many of the old manufacturing industries have relocated to places with cheaper labour, and service industries have grown. These economies are often described as post-industrial.

Asian economies grew the fastest at the start of the 21st century, and assumed an ever-growing share of global consumption. China in particular is set to become the world's largest economy by the middle of the century.

Post-industrial Society

Many believe that the rise of consumer culture significantly reshaped modern society, and that it stands behind many of the rapid and extensive cultural and economic shifts of the later 20th century.

I POPULARIZED THE TERM "POST-INDUSTRIAL SOCIETY", REFERRING TO A SOCIETY THAT IS DOMINATED BY CONSUMERS, WHOSE ESSENTIAL ATTITUDE IS THAT OF A HEDONISTIC CHASE AFTER INSTANT GRATIFICATION.

Daniel Bell

Influenced by the cultural criticism of capitalism, American sociologist **Daniel Bell** (1919–2011) saw culture, including lifestyle, fashion, media and sport, as the main output of a post-industrial society, generating ever more fads and lifestyles to cater for different consumers.

The distinction between production and consumption is blurred in a post-industrial society. This is most evident in the case of the internet, in which consumers create much of the content and do much of the advertising. Consumers are also a valuable source of information, helping with their feedback and input to design new products and updates.

Post Fordism

These developments towards service and knowledge economies have fundamentally changed the way that corporations work. These changes are often lumped together under the heading of "Post Fordism".

BUSINESSES NO LONGER ASPIRE TO THE MASS PRODUCTION OF IDENTICAL PRODUCTS. EMPHASIS HAS MOVED FROM QUANTITY AND VOLUME TO DIVERSITY AND SCOPE, LOOKING AT THE DIFFERENT NEEDS OF DIFFERENT CUSTOMERS. THIS RELIES HEAVILY ON INFORMATION AND SPECIALIZATION OF BOTH PRODUCTS AND JOBS, AND INVOLVES FREQUENT CHANGES IN THE LINE OF PRODUCTS.

As societies enter the post-industrial stage, the factors governing production and profit making change considerably.

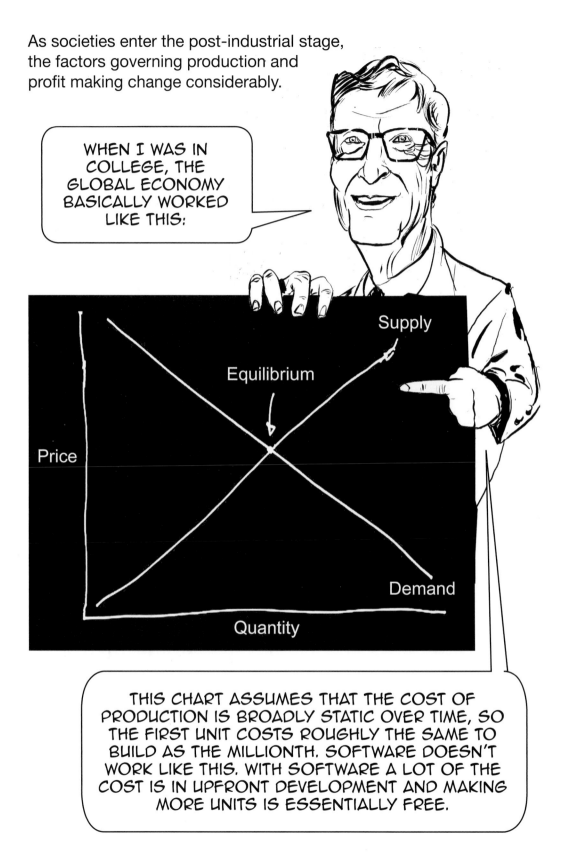

WHEN I WAS IN COLLEGE, THE GLOBAL ECONOMY BASICALLY WORKED LIKE THIS:

THIS CHART ASSUMES THAT THE COST OF PRODUCTION IS BROADLY STATIC OVER TIME, SO THE FIRST UNIT COSTS ROUGHLY THE SAME TO BUILD AS THE MILLIONTH. SOFTWARE DOESN'T WORK LIKE THIS. WITH SOFTWARE A LOT OF THE COST IS IN UPFRONT DEVELOPMENT AND MAKING MORE UNITS IS ESSENTIALLY FREE.

The Rise of Intangible Assets

Software is not the only type of asset that behaves differently to the production costs of physical goods, but it is one of the most prominent. It's indicative of a larger trend as advanced economies develop an ever greater reliance on so-called "**intangible assets**" – an economist's way of thinking about the changes that Bell was talking about.

BROADLY SPEAKING, TANGIBLE ASSETS ARE THINGS YOU CAN TOUCH: BUILDINGS, MACHINERY, VEHICLES. INTANGIBLE ASSETS ARE THINGS YOU CAN'T TOUCH LIKE SOFTWARE, DATABASES, PATENTS, MOVIES AND PIECES OF MUSIC, MARKET RESEARCH AND BRANDS. BUT IMPORTANTLY ALL OF THESE THINGS ARE DURABLE, WHICH IS TO SAY THEY CAN BE REUSED OVER TIME.

INTANGIBLES ARE BECOMING INCREASINGLY IMPORTANT. THIS IS A LONG-TERM TREND THAT HAS ONLY RECENTLY HIT ITS INFLECTION POINT.

Stian Westlake, British researcher on the social and economic impact of innovation

Jonathan Haskel, British economist

Scalability – the low cost of reproduction makes it cheap to reach customers (e.g. Google can make a change to its algorithm and deploy to millions of users at almost no incremental cost).

Sunkenness – most of the cost is paid upfront and is hard to recoup by other means (e.g. if a movie costs $150 million to make but flops at the box office, there's very little you can do to get return on that investment).

Spillovers – a lot of intangible investments are, broadly speaking, investments in ideas and can be easily copied by competitors (e.g. a single piece of music can be copyrighted in much of the world, but you can't copyright a musical genre).

Synergies – intangible investments become more valuable in the context of other intangible investments (e.g. Apple's design prowess has more economic power because Apple also has the expertise in how to put products together at scale and the brand to sell them).

For Haskel and Westlake, this shift towards intangible investment contributes to a number of long-term trends, including the infrastructure required to support this new economy and the rise of inequality. They called upon recent work which suggested that in the US between 1981–2013, over two thirds of income inequality could be explained by the difference between companies, and just one third could be explained by variations within firms (ignoring top executives at very large companies).

TO UNDERSTAND THE GROWTH IN INCOME INEQUALITY IT BECOMES CRUCIAL TO UNDERSTAND WHY SOME COMPANIES CAN PAY MORE THAN OTHERS.

THE RISE IN INTANGIBLES HELPS TO EXPLAIN HOW A FEW LEADING COMPANIES CAN DOMINATE AN INDUSTRY – LIKE TECHNOLOGY COMPANIES, HOLLYWOOD STUDIOS. THESE COMPANIES ARE BEST PLACED TO EXPLOIT THE SCALABILITY AND SPILLOVERS OF INTANGIBLES, WHICH MEANS THEY CAN BE MORE PRODUCTIVE AND BENEFIT FROM A VIRTUOUS CIRCLE. ULTIMATELY THIS MEANS THEY CAN PAY MORE TO GET THE PEOPLE THEY WANT – THOSE WHO CAN FIND SYNERGIES AND DRIVE MORE SCALE.

High revenues

Big budgets for special effects and Hollywood stars

Broad distribution to cinemas and streaming sites; merchandising deals

$10000000

SCRIPT

MEANWHILE WITHIN COMPANIES, IMPROVED BUSINESS PRACTICES (A DIFFERENT FLAVOUR OF INTANGIBLE ASSET) MEAN THAT SENIOR MANAGERS ARE ABLE TO FOCUS ON HIGHER VALUE TASKS AND THEIR PAY IS INCREASED AS A RESULT.

Further down the line, it is easy to think of technology replacing jobs. There have long been concerns about computers' ability to make certain roles obsolete.

THE COMPLICATING FACTOR IS THAT COMPUTERS AND SOFTWARE INVESTMENTS ARE VERY GOOD AT TAKING OVER REPETITIVE TASKS. LOW PAID JOBS (WAITING TABLES, CLEANING, CARE) FREQUENTLY DON'T INCLUDE MUCH ROUTINE, BUT MIDDLE INCOME JOBS TEND TO BE FULL OF ROTE TASKS.

David Autor
American economist

HOWEVER, HISTORY SHOWS THAT TECHNOLOGY CAN ALSO CHANGE THE TYPES OF JOBS THAT PEOPLE ARE ASKED TO DO, IMPROVING SALARIES IN THE PROCESS.

132

Readjusting to these new terms of post-Fordist production, corporations at the close of the 20th century became leaner, more flexible and adaptable to change. This also had a revolutionizing effect on the structure of employment, which turned into a "**gig economy**".

> A YOUNG NEW RECRUIT AT A FORDIST PLANT COULD REASONABLY LOOK FORWARD TO HIS GOLD WATCH AT RETIREMENT.

> IN THE POST-FORDIST ECONOMY, THE AVERAGE EMPLOYEE IS EXPECTED TO SWITCH JOBS REGULARLY AND ACQUIRE NEW SKILLS THROUGHOUT THEIR CAREER. A REGULAR WORKFORCE HAS BEEN SIGNIFICANTLY REPLACED BY OUTSOURCING, TEMPING AND OTHER FORMS OF SHORT-TERM EMPLOYMENT. UNEMPLOYMENT HAS MEANWHILE BECOME CHRONIC, PARTICULARLY AMONG UNSKILLED AND UNEDUCATED LABOUR.

133

Finance Capitalism

Hand in hand with the reduced importance of industry came a boom in the finance sector, which became a major element of the service economy. Some even refer to the current global economy as finance capitalism.

The Financial Daily

Economic policy since the 1980s caused a consolidation of international trade blocs and a sharp increase in the amount of capital held by multinational investment companies and institutional investors. These are financial companies that sit on trillions in pension funds, insurance money and the savings of millions of small investors.

These funds were entrusted to a handful of financial experts, who are thus always on the lookout for interesting investment opportunities. Increasingly more complicated financial instruments were invented to cater for them, which drew in more major players by their success.

Institutional investors came to own significant portions of major corporations which, no longer engaged mainly in the mass production of industrial goods, were only too happy to join in the search for alternative profit.

NO COMPANIES FIT THE BILL MORE THAN THE NEW HIGH TECH AND COMMUNICATIONS BUSINESSES, WHICH WERE CALLED THE "NEW ECONOMY" DURING THEIR MARKET BOOM IN THE LATE 1990S. HIGHLY DEPENDENT ON VENTURE CAPITAL, THEY QUICKLY ADOPTED NOVEL FINANCIAL DEVICES, FOR EXAMPLE, EMPLOYEE STOCK OPTIONS AS A MEANS OF PAYMENT.

THE WORLD OF FINANCE IS HIGHLY VOLATILE AND RENOWNED FOR MAKING BILLIONS VANISH LIKE MAGIC OVERNIGHT. ITS BEHAVIOUR WAS A MAJOR CAUSE OF THE DOT.COM BUBBLE BURST IN THE EARLY 2000S AND THE SUBPRIME CRISIS OF 2007–8, THE BIGGEST ECONOMIC CRISIS TO DATE SINCE THE GREAT DEPRESSION.

Global Shifts in Production

While advanced economies were becoming post-industrial and financialized, the production of goods has to happen somewhere. It moved mainly to Asian and Eastern European countries whose economies still rely heavily on the supply of labour and raw materials.

THE SCALE OF THIS TRANSFORMATION WAS UNPRECEDENTED AND SUDDEN. IN THE 1980S, BEFORE THE COLLAPSE OF THE USSR AND BEFORE CHINA AND INDIA MOVED TOWARDS MORE MARKET REFORMS, THE SIZE OF THE WORKFORCE PARTICIPATING IN THE GLOBAL ECONOMY WAS AROUND 1.46 BILLION WORKERS. THEN IN THE '90S CHINA, INDIA AND THE FORMER SOVIET BLOC OPENED UP MORE OR LESS SIMULTANEOUSLY; IN DOING SO THEY TOOK THE GLOBAL WORKFORCE TO AROUND 2.93 BILLION – ESSENTIALLY DOUBLING IT ALMOST OVERNIGHT.

Richard B. Freeman
American economist

The **BRICS** countries (Brazil, Russia, India, China and South Africa) account for over 40% of the world's population and have experienced impressive growth – despite some recent slowdown. Three are currently among the ten major global economies, with China leading the way. Particularly noteworthy is their establishment of the **New Development Bank** (NDB) in 2014 to rival the Western dominated World Bank.

THIS ECONOMIC GROWTH HAS RAISED OUR STANDARD OF LIVING, BUT WORKING AND LIVING CONDITIONS ARE STILL FAR BELOW WESTERN STANDARDS, LEVELS OF POVERTY AND CORRUPTION ARE HIGHER, AND IN SOME CASES HUMAN RIGHTS RECORDS ARE LESS THAN IMPRESSIVE.

Cultural Effects of Capitalism

But these have been economic concerns, and capitalism has attracted criticism for its cultural ramifications as much as its economic ones. Even before capitalism really got going, Adam Smith had suggested the need for free education to stop specialist workers doing repetitive jobs from becoming too stupid. Since then, critics have looked at everything from the environmental impact of the Industrial Revolution to the culture of consumerism that encourages people to keep spending.

Perhaps unsurprisingly, one of the foremost critics of the social effects of capitalism is Marx.

HIS VIEW ON THE ECONOMIC BASIS OF SOCIAL STRUCTURE ALLOWS HIM TO DEVELOP A CRITICISM OF THE WAY VARIOUS SOCIAL INSTITUTIONS OF CAPITALISM PRESERVE BOURGEOIS VALUES AND POWER STRUCTURES.

Max Weber and the Protestant Spirit

Influenced by Marx, though rejecting some of his main premisses, **Max Weber** (1864–1920) developed his social criticism of capitalism in the first decades of the 20th century.

I THOUGHT MARX WAS WRONG IN SEEING CULTURAL AND INTELLECTUAL PERSPECTIVES AS DETERMINED BY ECONOMICS.

IN PARTICULAR, I POINTED OUT THAT CAPITALISM EVOLVED ONLY IN PROTESTANT COUNTRIES, AND CONCLUDED THAT IT WAS IN FACT A RESULT OF THE PROTESTANT SPIRIT.

In *The Protestant Ethic and the Spirit of Capitalism* (1905), Weber claimed that there was a reason why capitalism did not evolve in Italy or Spain, for example, even though Italy produced the first significant merchant class and Spain the first empire. That reason was the Catholic religion, and not simply the material conditions of the economy.

Catholic and Protestant Ethics

In Catholicism, richness is a sin that is "tolerated".

THE CHURCH ITSELF WAS IMMENSELY RICH, SO RELIGIOUS PROTESTS THAT TENDED TO STRESS TOO MUCH WHAT JESUS SAID ABOUT THE RICH IN THE GOSPELS WERE SUPPRESSED.

BUT ON THE OTHER HAND, BEING WEALTHY WAS NEVER SEEN AS SOMETHING TO BE OPENLY PROUD OF, AND IF YOU DEVOTED YOUR LIFE TO IT YOU'D BE SCORNED.

In the Protestant ethics of the Calvinists and Puritans, things were exactly the opposite. Saving money and investing it rationally was seen as an almost religious duty. It was part of the overall religious project of exercising restraint and rational behaviour in all fields of life.

In Catholic countries it was alright to be draped in scarlet velvet, but wrong to be proud of your riches. And if you achieved your wealth through business alone, without having any political power, you'd still have to know your place.

IN PROTESTANT COUNTRIES IT WAS CONSIDERED WRONG TO SHOW OSTENTATIOUS SIGNS OF WEALTH (HENCE THE SUIT), BUT ATTENDING TO BUSINESS AND ECONOMIC SUCCESS WERE DEFINITELY SOMETHING TO BE PROUD OF.

Capitalism arose, according to Weber, as part of the overall Protestant project of **rationalizing** social existence. This project changed the face of social interaction and made it regulated, rational and bureaucratic. Managers run both public affairs and businesses alike.

The Rise of Rationality

For Weber, there are two related but different sorts of rationality that emerge from the Enlightenment and the Scientific Revolution.

The ideal liberal picture was of setting procedural rationality to serve the goals of moral rationality.

HOWEVER, IN REALITY THE OPPOSITE TOOK PLACE.

PROCEDURAL RATIONALITY BECAME AN END IN ITSELF – THE EFFICIENT AND REGULATED MANAGEMENT OF THE MARKET AND ALL SOCIAL ASPECTS BECAME THE GOAL, TO WHICH INDIVIDUAL LIVES ARE COMPLETELY SUBORDINATED.

In capitalism, profit becomes the goal of commercial organizations, and their employees and customers are considered as means to that effect. Management experts and campaign managers make their living by constantly supplying the need of organizations for more efficiency from their workers and higher sales from their customers.

143

Making Organizations Work for People

For Weber, it should always be remembered that organizations are meant to improve people's lives, and that means first of all that organizations deal with people, not with data and figures.

So the organization should be judged mainly according to how well it satisfies people in the framework of laws and guidelines. That would truly facilitate the freedom and autonomy of all individuals.

Neo-Marxism and the Frankfurt School

More extreme social critiques of capitalism follow Marx in claiming that the problem is with liberal ideology itself, not only with the way it was put into practice. During the Great Depression, the rise of fascism instead of the predicted communist revolution brought some Marxist theorists to analyse fascism as the last resort of capitalism, right before its inevitable collapse. These are the origins of neo-Marxist social thought during the 1930s.

THE LASTING IMPORTANCE OF NEO-MARXIST THEORIES HAS A LOT TO DO WITH THE WORK OF THE FRANKFURT SCHOOL OF THINKERS, WHICH CONCENTRATED AROUND THE FRANKFURT SCHOOL OF SOCIAL RESEARCH ONCE I BECAME ITS HEAD IN 1930.

Max Horkheimer
(1895–1973)

When the ground in Germany began to burn under the feet of this mostly Jewish circle of thinkers, they moved to New York and continued to work in Columbia University. It was mostly there that their thought really developed.

For the Frankfurt School, the heart of late post-industrial economies is the industrialization of culture. Culture becomes the main source of income in an age in which it is no longer a problem to supply mankind's material needs.

The Adoration of the New

Where physical conditions and material shortage no longer force people to work just to survive, the Frankfurt School saw a system of production that subordinates an entire population to the rules of its own mechanism, motivated by endless technological advance.

Goods have become completely disposable in an everlasting race in adoration of the new. All the while, using only a fraction of mankind's production capacity and working time in post-industrial economies, all the real needs of the population could be supplied.

Unmasking Consumer Culture

However, this transformation of "free time" is the reason why the struggle for the working day that Marx gives a lot of time to has become less of an issue in post-industrial economies.

The most important contribution of Horkheimer's neo-Marxist thought is his admission that material conditions alone cannot bring about the revolution. This breaks Marx's belief in a definite path to history. For Horkheimer, the only way beyond a post-industrial economy is for people to realize the totalitarian elements embedded in consumer culture – and this can be achieved only through education.

Adorno and the Media

Horkheimer's most famous student and collaborator, **Theodor Adorno** (1903–69), focused on the creation of global consumer culture.

FOR THE MASS MEDIA, LIKE POP MUSIC, HOLLYWOOD CINEMA AND COMMERCIAL TV, THE MASS CONSUMPTION OF ITS PRODUCTS IS THE BE ALL AND END ALL.

TO THAT END IT ENCOURAGES CELEBRITY WORSHIP AND FOCUS ON NEWS AND TRIVIA, WHICH ALLOWS IT TO KEEP PROVIDING THE SAME INSTANTLY GRATIFYING PRODUCTS IN EVER-CHANGING GUISES.

For Adorno, mass media forms the backbone of post-industrial economies, responsible for "intoxicating" the population and preventing them from improving their social situation. Not religion, but the media has become the "opium for the masses".

Herbert Marcuse

THE TECHNOLOGICAL AND SCIENTIFIC WAY OF THINKING BEHIND CAPITALIST SOCIETY IS THE VERY FOUNDATION OF THE PROBLEM.

THE WAY IN WHICH WE THINK ABOUT SOCIAL PROBLEMS MEANS THAT THE MOST SIGNIFICANT PROBLEMS CAN NEVER BE ADDRESSED.

The system of contemporary capitalism involves bureaucratic management, expert scientific analysis and statistically verifiable data. That system can study any problem and readjust to any demand as long as it can be scientifically and structurally defined.

151

Seeing Beyond the System

THROUGH MANAGEMENT, IT SEEMS, WE CAN SOLVE ANY PROBLEM.

THE ONE THING THAT CAN'T EVEN BE IMAGINED IN THIS WAY OF THINKING, THEN, IS A PROBLEM WITH RATIONAL MANAGEMENT ITSELF.

According to Marcuse, if we compare the life of average people through the years, then undoubtedly their lives today in material terms are much better then ever. They stand a better chance of being educated, housed, fed, and treated for disease. The one thing that the average person in the past had over the present is the recognition that social conditions are far from perfect.

IT IS THIS RECOGNITION THAT DROVE THE MASSES TO MAKE CHANGES AND IMPROVE THEIR STANDARD OF LIVING OVERALL OVER TIME.

The Situationists

Many of these ideas were taken on board by the Situationist International, a group of radical leftist thinkers and artists active between 1957 and 1972. One of the Situationists' most prolific and longest-serving authors was **Raoul Vaneigem** (b. 1934).

IT'S NOT ONLY CAPITALISM THAT FELL UNDER THE BOURGEOIS SPELL OF THE COMMODITY – THE SOVIET UNION, WITH ITS EMPHASIS ON INCREASING PRODUCTION EVEN THOUGH OUR BASIC NEEDS ARE FULFILLED, WAS AT BOTTOM A BOURGEOIS STATE.

AND THAT'S EVEN BEFORE YOU GET ONTO THE QUESTION OF THE RULING CLASS THAT CALLED ITSELF THE POLITBURO.

For the Situationists, like Horkheimer before them, the spread of the commodity, and the rise of leisure time used increasingly for economic activities, has resulted in everyone becoming proletarian.

Debord and the Spectacle

The group's theoretical critique of capitalism was developed most fully by **Guy Debord** (1931–94). Debord used the idea of the **spectacle** – broadly an updated version of Marx's concept of alienation with theatrical overtones – to analyse the role of the commodity in post-industrial economies.

ONCE GOODS ARE SO PLENTIFUL THAT THERE IS ENOUGH FOR EVERYONE, THEN USEFULNESS CEASES TO BE THE PRINCIPAL SOURCE OF VALUE, AND COMMODITY FETISHISM BECOMES WIDESPREAD.

THE RISE OF THE COMMODITY GIVES RISE TO THE SPECTACLE, AND THEN RELIES ON IT TO GIVE GOODS A SPECTACULAR VALUE THAT REPLACES THEIR USE VALUE.

These ideas find their most succinct expression in *Society of the Spectacle* (1967). For Debord, even rebellion becomes a commodity, as demonstrated by the products aimed at and sold to angsty teenagers. So it is that most of the debates of party politics and the theories of so-called alternative lifestyles are in fact doing nothing but offering the same basic system – they are nothing but a commodity in a new

Every Choice a Pseudo-choice

MODERN SOCIETY HAS ALREADY INVADED THE SOCIAL SURFACE OF EACH CONTINENT BY MEANS OF THE SPECTACLE.

IT DEFINES THE PROGRAMME OF THE RULING CLASS AND PRESIDES OVER ITS FORMATION.

JUST AS IT PRESENTS PSEUDO-GOODS TO BE COVETED, IT OFFERS FALSE MODES OF REVOLUTION TO LOCAL REVOLUTIONARIES.

Debord, *Society of the Spectacle,* § 57

As every choice becomes a pseudo-choice and mankind becomes increasingly alienated from reality, the result is that the world becomes banal. The more banal things become, the more the spectacle affirms their importance and vitality, the more it affirms that things are anything other than banal.

To counteract this, the Situationists staged a number of interventions and public acts. However, their concrete political actions did not spread much beyond publishing cartoons, vandalism and graffiti.

Down with a world in which the guarantee that we will not die of starvation has been purchased with the guarantee that we will die of boredom.

AGAINST SLEEP AND NIGHTMARE #6

When the Situationist International disbanded in 1972, it had just two remaining members. The rest had either resigned or been thrown out, often as a result of a disagreement with Debord. Even Vaneigem, who left in 1970 citing personal and group failures, attracted a scathing response. In 1988, Debord published *Comments on the Society of the Spectacle*, in which he says that the spectacle has become so powerful that resistance to it is no longer possible. He committed suicide in 1994.

Right-wing Critiques of Capitalism

The claim that capitalism has led to the impoverishment of life is neither new nor unique to critics on the left. Among conservative critics the same idea has a long tradition, for reasons including the belief that capitalism is taking us away from the spiritual life and has led to the breakdown of traditional values. This was the cause of the Luddite social movement, which during 1811–12 led attacks against the industrialized textile mills in Britain of the early Industrial Revolution.

More recently, this line of thought has found clear expression in the philosophy of **Martin Heidegger** (1889–1976).

THE SPIRIT OF TECHNOLOGY LIES AT THE HEART OF MODERN EXISTENCE.

TECHNOLOGICAL THINKING TAKES EVERYTHING IN THE WORLD TO BE RAW MATERIAL – SOMETHING WHOSE ONLY WORTH LIES IN WHAT CAN BE MADE OF IT.

IN OTHER WORDS, TECHNOLOGICAL THINKING IS PURELY NIHILISTIC.

Capitalist thinking is just as nihilistic as technological thinking, because in capitalism nothing has an intrinsic value beyond its exchange value on the market. All essential distinctions between different occupations and lifestyles disappear, as they all merge into the capitalist market and lifestyle.

Knowing Your Place

The conservative criticism of modernity and capitalism yearns, to a degree, for social conditions that existed before modernity. In agricultural societies, a person's environment, culture, profession and social status were all integrated. For each person, the world and their place in it were imbued with sense and value, and social life was a complete whole that was nevertheless localized and historical.

IN MODERNITY IT IS THE OPPOSITE. NO MATTER WHERE YOU ARE, YOU ARE ALWAYS PART OF A FLUID GLOBAL CULTURE THAT'S NOT RELATED TO ANY LOCATION, HISTORY OR VALUE SYSTEM.

WHATEVER VALUE LIFE MAY HAVE HAD HAS BEEN COMPLETELY TAKEN OVER BY MASS CULTURE THAT PERVADES ALL AREAS OF LIFE.

Leo Strauss (1899–1973) took the discussion into the field of politics.

I DENOUNCED MODERN LIBERAL AND CAPITALIST THINKING BECAUSE IT RESTS ON THE STRICT FACT-VALUE DISTINCTION (THE DISTINCTION BETWEEN WHAT **IS** AND WHAT **OUGHT TO BE**) AND REMOVES VALUES FROM POLITICS AND ECONOMICS.

I CALLED FOR A RETURN TO A MORE ANCIENT GREEK CONCEPTION OF POLITICS, AS RESPONSIBLE FOR THE "GOOD LIFE" OF ALL CITIZENS – A LIFE OF VALUE.

Scientific and technological management of society is the very root of the problem, according to the conservative critique. What is needed is a deep philosophical understanding of the purpose of mankind and concepts like justice, nobility and the good life. Among the many freedoms that the liberal state is so proud of, there should be the freedom not to live like the bourgeois urban type.

MODERN SOCIETY AND CAPITALIST THINKING, THAT ORIGINATED WITH HOBBES AND LOCKE, ARE FOUNDED ON THE BASEST ELEMENTS OF HUMANITY – DESIRE, EGOTISM AND GREED. MODERNITY SHOULD INCORPORATE A DISCUSSION OF THE VALUE OF LIFE THAT PREVAILED IN ANTIQUITY.

Politics should come to rest again on an understanding of human nature and value, and allowing every person the room for intellectual development and self-fulfilment.

In short, what conservative thinkers are calling for is an ideological revolution, not a material one. They do not wish to change the way goods are distributed, but rather to displace management, technology and progress as the principal values of modern society. This should be achieved mainly through education and intellectual influence on elite groups holding key positions in society – such as intellectuals, religious institutions and the government.

Feminist Critiques of Capitalism

In 1988 New Zealand economist **Marilyn Waring** published *If Women Counted*. It was not the first book to put an economic value on women's unpaid labour, but it helped inspire a movement to better understand the role of unpaid work.

TRADITIONAL NATIONAL ACCOUNTING SYSTEMS TYPICALLY IGNORE THE ECONOMIC VALUE OF THE CARE AND REPRODUCTIVE WORK TRADITIONALLY DONE BY WOMEN – SUCH AS CHILD CARE, DOMESTIC COOKING, LAUNDRY AND EVEN BREASTFEEDING. PUTTING A MONETARY VALUE TO IT WAS A WAY TO MAKE IT VISIBLE FOR POLICY MAKING PURPOSES, FOR FAIRNESS AND EQUALITY.

Many of the traditional critics of capitalism have similarly ignored this aspect of labour, and have often been prone themselves to a patriarchal picture of gender roles.

MARXISTS TEND TO FOCUS ON THINGS THAT ARE CLASSICALLY MEASURED IN ECONOMICS, NOTABLY THE MANUFACTURE OF GOODS AND THE EXPLOITATION OF THE WORKFORCE THAT CREATES THOSE GOODS.

LOOKING AT THINGS THIS WAY SYSTEMICALLY IGNORES THE "PERENNIAL BASIS" ON WHICH THE CAPITALIST SYSTEM IS BUILT. WITHOUT THE PROPAGATION OF THE SPECIES AND OTHER FORMS OF DOMESTIC LABOUR YOU CANNOT HAVE A CAPITALIST SYSTEM.

Maria Mies, German sociologist

Unpaid Work

ONCE YOU START LOOKING AT THE VALUE OF UNPAID WORK, IT STARTS TO ALTER YOUR VIEW OF ECONOMIC GROWTH.

THE WAVE OF GROWTH IN GDP THAT FOLLOWED FROM WOMEN'S INCREASED PARTICIPATION IN THE WORKPLACE, WHICH GAINED MOMENTUM IN THE 1960S, STARTS TO LOOK INFLATED ONCE YOU REALIZE THAT THE VALUE OF WORK IN THE HOME HAS BEEN IGNORED.

THE REALITY IS THAT GDP IS JUST NOT A GOOD MEASURE OF THE REAL ECONOMY. AND THERE ARE SIGNIFICANT RISKS TO LOOKING ONLY AT WHAT CAN BE TRADED, RATHER THAN TAKING A HOLISTIC VIEW OF WHAT IS PRODUCED INCLUDING THAT WHICH IS PRODUCED AND USED IN THE HOME.

Domestic labour in most countries is disproportionately – although not exclusively – done by women. Some countries, such as Norway, have started trying to evaluate this often ignored part of the economy as performed by the entire population.

Sustainability

A growing number of critics have voiced concern that the constant demand for economic growth, and corresponding production of ever more goods required for investors to see a return on their capital, is incompatible with care for the environment. One line of criticism says that where capitalism requires constant growth and ever more production, eventually we will dig ourselves into an irreversible environmental catastrophe. This line of thought is in the direct tradition of **Thomas Malthus** (1766–1834) who worried that if the population kept expanding, humanity would have no way to feed itself.

IN THE END HUMANITY DID FIND WAYS TO FEED ITS EXPANDING POPULATION, AS TECHNOLOGY ALLOWED FARMING TO BECOME MORE PRODUCTIVE. BUT THERE WAS NO WAY I COULD HAVE FORESEEN THIS.

Modern Malthusian criticisms of capitalism suffer from a similar problem to Malthus's original prediction – technological innovations have repeatedly proven very effective at boosting productivity. Sometimes these productivity gains have come at great environmental cost, such as how modern fishing techniques have caused significant depletion of fish stocks. At other times they have allowed us to lower our environmental impact through efficiency gains.

THE CURRENT TREND IS TOWARDS EVER GREATER LEVELS OF CONSUMPTION, AND THESE MAY PROVE TO BE UNSUSTAINABLE IN THE LONG RUN. BUT THAT DOESN'T MEAN THAT UNSUSTAINABLE CONSUMPTION IS FUNDAMENTAL TO CAPITALISM. AT ITS ROOT CAPITALISM IS ABOUT SEEING A RETURN ON INVESTMENTS IN CAPITAL. THIS MEANS THAT CHANGES IN GOVERNMENT POLICY COULD POTENTIALLY AVOID A CONSUMPTION-DRIVEN CATASTROPHE - FOR EXAMPLE, BY CHANGING THE WAY COMPANIES ARE TAXED SO THERE ARE MORE EFFECTIVE WAYS OF MAKING PROFIT THAN SIMPLY PRODUCING MORE AND MORE GOODS WITH NO ATTENTION TO THE ENVIRONMENT.

WE COULD, FOR EXAMPLE, PUT HIGH TAXES ON DANGEROUS EMISSIONS FROM MANUFACTURING.

A more subtle environmentalist critique of capitalism is that while progress has been made in accounting for the economic impact of human activity on the environment, the standard analyses do not go far enough, because they focus on what has been made and what can be easily counted.

> CAPITALIST ECONOMICS VALUES EXTRACTED AND PROCESSED RESOURCES, TRADABLE GOODS AND MARKETABLE SERVICES MORE THAN CONSERVED GOODS AND UN-USED SERVICES (IN MUCH THE SAME WAY THAT IT IGNORES THE ECONOMIC ROLE OF FREE LABOUR IN THE HOME).

Sabine O'Hara, American academic

This systemic bias means that it is harder to value the conserved rainforest which superficially produces nothing, than it is to value the cattle farm which replaces it. This is despite the fact that oxygen from the rainforests is needed to support life as we know it; it is extremely *valuable* but not economically *valued*. Thus, an economic world view that is fundamentally a capitalist world view risks biasing policy decisions that could benefit the world's population.

John Rawls (1921–2002) revived academic interest in political philosophy and the question of the social justice of capitalism in English-speaking countries with his book *A Theory of Justice* (1971). In it, Rawls tries to solve the long-standing problem of the fair distribution of goods using the idea of a social contract.

The original position uses the idea that if you are ignorant of your own self-interest, the only thing you can do is act fairly, because it is only by acting fairly that you minimize the risks to yourself – *ignorance models impartiality.*

What Rawls is really asking is:

Rawls' answer is that from the original position we'd choose a society that minimized personal risk, as self-interest would steer us away from situations that might result in us ending up as slaves.

Liberty and Difference

Rawls thinks that from the original position all rational people would choose the following basic principles.

*1. Each person is to have an equal right to the most extensive basic liberty compatible with a similar liberty for others (the **liberty principle**).*

2. Social and economic inequalities are to be arranged so that:
a) offices and positions must be open to everyone under conditions of fair equality of opportunity;
*b) they are to be of the greatest benefit to the least-advantaged members of society (the **difference principle**).*

The difference principle says that social inequalities are justified only if they help the worst-off in society more than any other way of distributing goods.

The liberty principle represents Rawls' loyalty to liberalism and a generally capitalist framework. The difference principle represents his revision of classical liberalism and his attempt to integrate it anew with social justice.

THE PRACTICAL IMPLICATIONS OF THE DIFFERENCE PRINCIPLE ARE THE ECONOMIC POLICY TYPICAL OF THE MODERN WELFARE STATE ...

PROGRESSIVE TAXATION AND OTHER ECONOMIC FACTORS PAY FOR BETTER PUBLIC EDUCATION, HEALTH, TRANSPORT AND EMPLOYMENT CONDITIONS.

Although Rawls' views are about as left as liberal thinking gets, they should not be confused with socialism. The main difference is that Rawls does not take equality and the reduction of social gaps as an end in itself. It does not matter, for Rawls, if there is gross inequality in the population, as long as the worst-off benefit from this.

Nozick and Right-wing Libertarianism

Criticisms of Rawls' theory include pointing out that the original position might not be as Rawls presents it – it might not be as neutral as he maintains, and might stack the deck towards modern, individualistic social structures. Perhaps Rawls' best-known critic is his Harvard colleague **Robert Nozick** (1938–2002). In his book *Anarchy, State and Utopia* (1974), he argues in favour of right-wing libertarianism.

IN OTHER WORDS, I BELIEVE THAT PEOPLE HAVE A NUMBER OF RIGHTS – THE RIGHT TO LIFE, PRIVATE PROPERTY, ETC. – AND THAT THE STATE SHOULD STAY OUT OF PEOPLE'S LIVES EXCEPT TO ENSURE THOSE RIGHTS.

TO ME, ANY REDISTRIBUTIVE SYSTEM IMPINGES ON PEOPLE'S LIBERTY.

Taxation as Forced Labour?

For Nozick, it is entirely right that Wilt makes more money, because people have entered into the agreement freely. Moreover, he thinks that it is just regardless of what pattern is chosen for the distribution of goods before Wilt puts his box out.

Nozick thinks that this is sufficient to establish the idea that any system that demands that the distribution of goods has to fit a particular pattern is wrong because it impinges on people's liberty. So it is that "a socialist society would have to forbid capitalist acts between consenting adults".

But, as some of Nozick's critics have pointed out, the loss of liberty for those paying tax often results in an increase in liberty for the poor, who benefit from things like access to free education.

The sort of rights and freedoms that Nozick acknowledges are things like the right to life – i.e. negative rights that specifically restrain people from causing harm – rather than positive rights to aid and assistance, like a right to education. Nozick proposes a minimal state.

THE CORRECT ROLE OF THE STATE IS TO PROTECT US FROM EACH OTHER AND FROM EXTERNAL THREAT.

THE STATE IS JUSTIFIED ONLY IN SO FAR AS IT SAFEGUARDS RIGHTS AND PROTECTS PEOPLE AGAINST FORCE, FRAUD, AND THEFT, AND ENFORCES CONTRACTS.

THE STATE ITSELF UNACCEPTABLY VIOLATES PEOPLE'S RIGHTS IF IT ATTEMPTS TO DO ANY MORE THAN THIS.

With a set-up like this, it seems likely that Nozick's utopia will rapidly develop into some sort of brutal 19th-century capitalism.

Fukuyama and the End of History

Marx was not the only thinker to see capitalism through the prism of Hegel. **Francis Fukuyama** (b. 1952) also uses the idea that history – viewed as the process of human development – will stop. But instead of stopping with communism, Fukuyama believes that it ends with capitalism and liberal democracy. He famously put this view forward in a book called *The End of History and the Last Man* (1992).

THE TITLE IS A HEGELIAN JOKE ...

THE MOST COMMON MISTAKE IS TO THINK THAT BY "HISTORY" I MEAN EVENTS, WHEN I MEANT TO SAY THAT LIBERAL DEMOCRACY IS THE HIGHEST DEVELOPMENT OF MANKIND'S POLITICAL IDEOLOGY.

But unlike Marx, Fukuyama agrees with Hegel's remark that history ended in 1806, because by then the ideological framework of the French and American revolutions was already in place. Of course, people came up with new ideas afterwards, but for Fukuyama, none of them represents any real progress on liberal democracy.

Writing in the late 1990s, Fukuyama made much of his empirical case – in the 19th century very few countries could be called democratic, whereas on the verge of the 21st century the great majority of governments made some claim to democracy.

EVEN STATES THAT MAINTAINED STRICT AUTHORITARIAN RULE, LIKE THE FORMER EAST GERMANY, PAID LIP SERVICE TO DEMOCRATIC IDEALS.

AND AS IT BECAME CLEAR THAT THE MARXIST RHETORIC OF FREEDOM DID NOT LIVE UP TO THE FREEDOM DELIVERED BY WESTERN DEMOCRACY, THE IDEOLOGICAL BATTLE WAS WON AS THE BERLIN WALL FELL.

Directional History

But the apparent victory of democracy and capitalism at the end of the 1980s and the beginning of the 1990s could well just be an accident of events. To claim that they are the end of history, Fukuyama needs to provide a mechanism that explains why history is leading up to them.

Fukuyama approaches this from two angles: the first is an argument from natural science designed to show that human history is **directional**.

THE ARGUMENT CAN BE BRIEFLY SUMMARIZED AS FOLLOWS ...

THE END OF HISTORY

1. Natural science is one area where people can definitely be said to make progress – Newton was a brilliant physicist, but it is quite correct to say that today's undergraduate understands more about the world than Newton did.

2. Natural science shapes societies by giving military and economic advantages: military and economic success mean that countries must match the technology and often production techniques of their neighbours.

3. In effect this is industrialization, as it involves more than just bringing technology into the workplace – it involves rationalizing the division of labour, and the transportation of goods, i.e. the essence of efficient capitalism.

However, this argument is not enough to get Fukuyama to the claim that capitalism is the end of history. For that he needs a second argument, and this requires two more ideas:

1. THAT SCIENTIFIC IDEAS, ONCE INVENTED, CANNOT BE UN-INVENTED — MEANING THAT ULTIMATELY PROGRESS IS ONE-WAY.

2. THAT HUMANITY WILL NEVER COME UP WITH A BETTER WAY OF PRODUCING GOODS THAN CAPITALISM.

That gets us to capitalism. However, establishing capitalism bundled with democracy as the final stage in the evolutionary process needs yet another argument. After all, in economic terms a market-orientated dictatorship might well be more efficient than a democracy, as it has less need to appease the people.

The Struggle for Recognition

LIKE MARX, I TOOK THE IDEA THAT HISTORY IS **DIALECTICAL**, COMPOSED OF THE STRUGGLE BETWEEN MASTER AND SLAVE, AND THAT HISTORY ENDS WHEN THESE TWO POLES ARE COMBINED.

UNLIKE MARX, I TOOK FROM HEGEL AND HIS INTERPRETER **ALEXANDRE KOJÈVE** (1902–68) THE IDEA THAT THIS WAS REALLY A STRUGGLE FOR RECOGNITION. SPECIFICALLY THE STRUGGLE FOR OTHERS TO RECOGNIZE US AS EQUALS.

For Fukuyama, we recognize others as equals when we allow them equality under the law and the ability to participate in the decision-making process. In other words, it is the basics of liberal democracy that dissolves the tension between master and slave, because it grants equal rights and the ability to vote. Democracy, therefore, is also the end of history.

Challenging the Free Market

Where Fukuyama's argument draws strength from the idea that capitalism is the most efficient way of producing goods, more recently economists like Nobel Prize-winners **George Akerlof** (b. 1940) and **Joseph Stiglitz** (b. 1943) have begun to look into this idea more rigorously.

Their work challenges Adam Smith's idea that became one of the lynchpins of classical and neo-classical economics – that it is free markets that allow production and economies to thrive.

Joseph Stiglitz

BUT THIS IDEA RESTS ON THE ASSUMPTION THAT MARKETS WORK WITH PERFECT INFORMATION, AND IN TRUTH THIS IS ALMOST NEVER THE CASE.

MANAGERS WILL OFTEN KNOW MORE ABOUT HOW A COMPANY IS BEHAVING THAN ITS SHAREHOLDERS, SELLERS WILL OFTEN KNOW MORE THAN BUYERS ABOUT THE QUALITY OF THEIR GOODS, ETC.

The Developing World: Free Trade … ?

In Stiglitz's hands, this simple idea has become a broad programme for how economies in the developing world should be nurtured.

… or State Capitalism?

South Korea today is democratic, prosperous and developed. But it got there not by chasing free trade but with something more like state capitalism.

> THIS INCLUDED: A SYSTEM OF PROTECTIONIST TARIFFS; JUDICIOUS REINVESTMENT OF GOVERNMENT FUNDS IN EDUCATION AND INFRASTRUCTURE; AND DIRECT GOVERNMENT INVOLVEMENT IN THE STEEL INDUSTRY.

> IN MUCH OF AFRICA, THE ECONOMIES WERE STRUGGLING IN THE 1980S, SO WE TURNED TO THE WORLD BANK FOR HELP.

> WHILE WE GOT INVESTMENT, IT CAME WITH A NUMBER OF CONDITIONS, INCLUDING UNREALISTIC REPAYMENT SCHEMES AND OPENING OUR MARKETS TO WESTERN GOODS WHEN WE HAD NOTHING TO SELL IN RETURN.

Crucially, direct government investment of exactly the sort that worked in Korea was prohibited.

185

UN sponsored programmes, such as the Heavily Indebted Poor Countries Initiative, encouraged economic growth and development across the continent, leading to a reduction of national debts. This is particularly felt along the coasts, aided by the discovery of new oil reserves in the oceans. Stronger economies, such as those of Ghana, Kenya and Nigeria, were also able to rely increasingly on domestic debt and on loans from the BRICS countries provided without the conditions imposed by Western-led organizations.

MANY AFRICAN COUNTRIES, THOUGH, CONTINUE TO BE BURDENED BY LARGE NATIONAL DEBT, FEW OPTIONS FOR FINANCIALIZATION AND ECONOMIES RELYING HEAVILY ON THE SUPPLY OF RAW MATERIALS FOR THE INDUSTRIES AND MARKETS OF THE DEVELOPED WORLD. AFRICA IS STILL THE POOREST CONTINENT BY FAR, WITH A TOTAL GDP OF ABOUT A THIRD OF THE US'S.

I FIND IT STAGGERING THAT, DESPITE THESE EXAMPLES, PEOPLE STILL INSIST THAT FREE TRADE IS THE BEST WAY TO HELP DEVELOPMENT. FOR ME IT JUST MISUNDERSTANDS THE WAY THAT MARKETS WORK – THEY ARE BY THEIR VERY NATURE UNEVEN.

Stiglitz is not without critics. Perhaps the most obvious alternative to his views on development is to accept that the interventionist policies in South Korea worked, but to view them as a necessary response to Western governments insisting on open borders for Western goods in developing countries, while maintaining their own system of tariffs and subsidies for industries like agriculture.

On this broadly neo-liberal view, the problem is not that free trade is bad for development, but that free trade has never been given a chance. It is similarly open to neo-liberals to accept the idea that asymmetrical information creates instability, but to think that the correct way to deal with this is not more government intervention, but less – and that governments should focus on trying to even out those disparities of information

Islam and Capitalism

Capitalism continues to spread
untouched by all this theorizing,
and one of its biggest growth areas
is Sharia banking (banking that
conforms to Islamic law). Like the
Bible, the Koran takes a dim view of
charging interest.

*Thou shalt not charge interest to your brother, interest of money,
interest of goods, interest on anything that you have lent.*

Deuteronomy XXIII:19

*That which you lend out for profit through the property of [other]
people, will have no increase with Allah. But that which you give out
for charity, seeking God's pleasure, will increase: it is this that will get
a reward many fold.*

Koran, Ar-Room:39

But today, Muslims often take a more serious view of this commandment
than Christians, which has resulted in a number of ingenious adaptations
of traditional capitalist tools.

Sharia Banking

The standard way of financing trade is known as *murabaha*.

A MANUFACTURER IN NEED OF RAW MATERIALS WILL ASK A BANK TO BUY THESE ON HIS BEHALF.

IF THE BANK DECIDES IT'S A GOOD INVESTMENT, IT WILL THEN BUY THE GOODS AND CHARGE THE COMPANY A SERVICE CHARGE, WHICH IS JUSTIFIED ON THE GROUNDS THAT THE GOODS MIGHT SPOIL WHILE IN THE BANK'S POSSESSION.

Murabaha can also be paid back in instalments, after the goods have been delivered, so economically this works for banks in an almost identical way to charging interest. Things like cars can be bought on a lend-lease basis – at the end of the lease period, once the bank has made its money, the goods are transferred to their new owner.

The emergence of Islamic capitalism, like the rise of greater industrial efficiency in the 19th century in countries that lacked an empire, is typical of capitalism's flexibility and, by extension, its instability. After all, if things were entirely stable, then new developments could not supersede the established way of doing things. For Adam Smith, the instability of capitalism and free markets both facilitated and was kept in check by the "invisible hand".

Bursting the Bubble

However, that instability can also throw things off balance. As far back as the 1630s, the early pioneers managed to develop what is now often regarded as the first example of a speculative bubble.

While economists debate the true significance of the tulip bubble, what is clear is that the history of capitalism is littered with such sharp market "corrections". They are a feature of capitalist systems, and there are no known surefire ways to avoid them. What varies is the effect they have on the wider economy and the turmoil they bring to people's lives, but at their worst they can devastate the global economy, bringing poverty and hardship to millions.

There is no shortage of recent examples of the erratic market behaviour of capitalism. Financial bubbles and various forms of recklessness brought about a series of setbacks during the first decade of the 21st century, leading to the **subprime crisis**, which drove many countries into debt when called to bail out their failing financial system. The recession that followed did not help these economies recuperate and it also drove unemployment up. Eventually talk of some countries defaulting on their debts led to a wide implementation of strict austerity plans across the Western world.

THESE SETBACKS AND RECESSIONS JOINED THE WIDENING SOCIOECONOMIC GAPS, WORSENING EMPLOYMENT CONDITIONS, MEDIAN WAGE STAGNATION AND RISING UNEMPLOYMENT DURING DECADES OF PRIVATIZATION, GLOBALIZATION AND DEREGULATION OF THE MARKETS. INDIVIDUAL COUNTRIES WERE HELPLESS TO COMBAT THESE ISSUES BECAUSE OF THEIR COMMITMENT TO INTERNATIONAL TRADE AGREEMENTS. THIS FINALLY LED TO A POLITICAL BACKLASH ALSO FELT HIGHER UP THE SOCIOECONOMIC LADDER, AND IS ONE CRUCIAL REASON FOR THE ISOLATIONIST DRIVE SIGNIFIED BY EVENTS LIKE BREXIT AND MY ELECTION AS PRESIDENT.

All Things Not Being Equal

Advances in computing have helped modern economic historians to understand the long-term development of the global economy in a way that was simply unavailable to their predecessors.

To arrive at this general rule, French economist **Thomas Piketty** used in-depth analysis of the economic development of the USA, UK and France and topped it up with other markets when data were available.

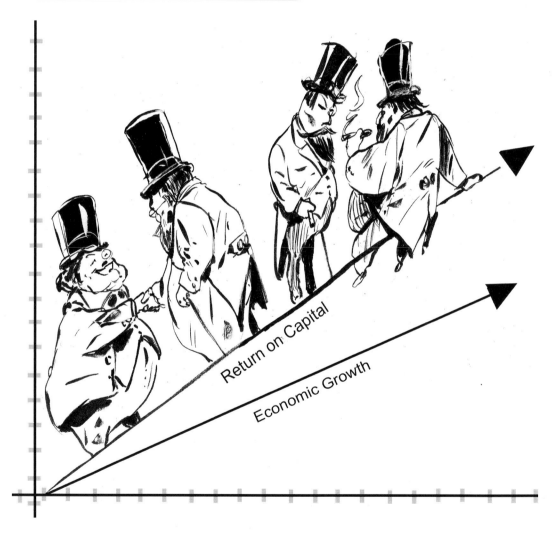

Piketty argues that the exception to this general rule is when an economy receives a shock that pushes it towards a more egalitarian mode of distribution, such as in the periods following both World Wars.

When return on capital grows faster than economic growth the wealthy get wealthier as the return on capital is not just used as income but also grows the underlying stock of capital. Taking a long-term view, without corrective action, this means that **inherited wealth** becomes increasingly important.

In France and the UK there has long been awareness of the power of inherited wealth. America was insulated from its power because of population growth from immigration and a higher birth rate – expansion factors that are now in decline. Inherited wealth tends to be less important in any market that is growing quickly.

There are those who feel that Piketty's analysis suffers from a variety of problems.

FOR ME AND MANY OTHERS, PIKETTY'S DECISION TO INCLUDE HOUSING AND LAND IN HIS DEFINITION OF CAPITAL IS A WEAKNESS IN HIS ANALYSIS, BECAUSE THEIR INCREASE ACCOUNTS FOR MUCH OF THE LONG-TERM TREND HE'S DESCRIBING.

THE PROJECT OF FORMULATING GENERAL LAWS IN ECONOMICS IS PROBLEMATIC, AND TYPICALLY OF LOW EXPLANATORY VALUE BECAUSE OF THE IMPACT OF LOCAL HISTORICAL, POLITICAL AND INSTITUTIONAL CONTEXTS.

Daron Acemoglu
Turkish-American economist

CAPITAL
Thomas Piketty

ANOTHER CONCERN WITH PIKETTY'S WORK IS THAT HE ASSUMES A BROADLY CONSTANT RATE OF RETURN, BUT AS THE SUPPLY OF CAPITAL INCREASES THE RETURN ON EVERY DOLLAR INVESTED SHOULD DIMINISH.

Some of Piketty's data have also been questioned as newer information has become available. However, the data which show that inequality has been rising since the 1980s within Western economies have not been seriously contested.

Further Reading

Smith, A., *The Wealth of Nations*, 1776. Smith's classic, and the launch pad for much of subsequent economics; surprisingly readable.

Hobbes, T., *Leviathan, or the Matter, Forme, and Power of a Commonwealth, Ecclesiastical and Civil* (commonly referred to as *Leviathan*), 1651. Early-modern masterpiece of political thought.

Locke, J., *Second Treatise on Government*, 1689. Locke's outline for a civil society; covers a lot of ground in a relatively small number of pages (the first Treatise is little read by anyone other than Locke scholars).

Mill, J.S., *On Liberty*, 1859, and *Utilitarianism*, 1863. Mill's two classics; *On Liberty* looks at the individual's rights in the face of the state, and grounds these rights on the utility principle which is discussed further in *Utilitarianism*.

Ricardo, D., *Principles of Political Economy and Taxation*, 1817. A key work in the development of the science of economics in general, and the first rigorous formulation of "classical" 19th-century economics.

Keynes, J.M., *General Theory of Employment, Interest and Money*, Macmillan Press, 1936. Considered by many Keynes' most complete work, in which he lays down his most developed account of his economic theory concerning the fluctuations of the capitalist market and the way to control them.

History

Runciman, S., *A History of the Crusades*, Peregrine Books, 1951–4. Republished in Penguin; three-volume history of the crusades.

Berlin, I., *Many Thousands Gone, The First Two Centuries of Slavery in North America*, Harvard University Press, 1998.

Brook, T. and Wakabayashi, B.T., *Opium Regimes: China, Britain, and Japan, 1839–1952*, University of California Press, 2000.

Thorold, P., *The London Rich: The Creation of a Great City from 1666 to the Present*, Viking, 1999. A look at the history of London that follows the flow of income.

Hobsbawm, E.J., *The Age of Revolution: Europe, 1789–1848*, new edition, Abacus 1988. *The Age of Capital, 1848–1875*, new edition, Abacus, 1988. *The Age of Empire, 1875–1914*, new edition, Abacus, 1989. Three-volume study of the turbulent 19th century.

Friedman, M. and Schwartz , A.J., *Monetary History of the United States, 1867–1960*, Princeton University Press, 1963. Contains Friedman's famous assessment of the causes of the Great Depression.

Woodham-Smith, C., *The Great Hunger, Ireland 1845–1849*, HarperCollins, 1962, reprinted in Penguin. History of the the Irish famine.

Weber and Marx

Weber, M., *The Protestant Ethic and the Spirit of Capitalism, and Other Writings*, Penguin, 2002. Outlines his view of the connection between capitalism, conceptions of rationality and efficiency, and the Protestant ethics.

Marx, K., *Capital, Vol. 1: A Critique of Political Economy*, Pelican Books, 1976. This is Marx's most developed account of the development and workings of capitalism, as well as its inevitable demise.

Tucker, Robert C. (ed.), *The Marx–Engels Reader*, W.W. Norton, 1978. A collection of writings from all periods of Marx's creative thinking, showing the development of his thought from philosophy towards eonomic theory.

Hegel, G.F.W., *Elements of the Philosophy of Right*, 1821, and *Lectures on the Philosophy of History*, 1837.

Neo-Marxism

Marcuse, H., *The One Dimensional Man*, second edition, Routledge, 1991. Marcuse's last work, containing his vision of contemporary society and the "dictatorship of freedom" of the rational-scientific-bureaucratic system in control of it.

Debord, G., *Society of the Spectacle*, 1967; English translation, *Black and Red*, 1970, revised 1977. A classic of late 20th-century Marxism, the prose can be dense and technical (this edition is preferable to the Nicholson-Smith translation from Zone).

Debord, G., *Comments on the Society of the Spectacle*, 1989; new English edition, Verso, 1998. Pessimistic evaluation of the inescapable power of the spectacle.

Adorno, T. and Horkheimer, M., *Dialectics of Enlightenment*, new edition, Verso, 1997. Analysis of the effects of the scientific revolution on society. The "rational" tendency to reduce everything to quantifiable, operational terms results in the degrading of everything that cannot be quantified this way, including the worth of the individual, interpersonal relationships, and morality.

Adorno, T., *The Culture Industry*, Routledge, 1991. Adorno's most comprehensive analysis of mass media as the industrialization of entertainment and art, which become instruments of consumer culture.

Vaneigem, R., *The Revolution of Everyday Life*, second English edition, Rebel Press, 1983. Less technical and more accessible than Debord's *Society of the Spectacle*; a good place to start with Situationist thought.

Conservatism

Heidegger, M., *The Question Concerning Technology and Other Essays*, Harper Perennial, 1982. This is Heidegger at his most readable form, discussing the metaphysical dimension of technology, science and mathematics, via excursions into Greek and Modern philosophy.

Strauss, L., *What is Political Philosophy? and Other Studies*, University of Chicago Press, 1988. A brilliant collection of essays in which Strauss lays out his unique understanding of political philosophy and the role of the philosopher in society. Strauss purports to solve the deep paradoxes of contemporary liberalism by recourse to the Greek conception of politics.

Contemporary Commentary

Rawls, J., *A Theory of Justice*, 1972, second revised edition, Oxford University Press, 1999. Reinvigorated academic political philosophy in the 1970s; has become something of a modern classic for the liberal-left.

Nozick, R., *Anarchy, State and Utopia*, Blackwell, 1974. Often put on undergraduate political reading lists right after Rawls for balance – a clarion call for the libertarian right.

Fukuyama, F., *The End of History and the Last Man*, Penguin, 1992. Basically a bourgeois-Marxist utopia – perhaps more read and quoted than academically admired.

Stiglitz, J., *Making Globalisation Work,* Penguin Allen Lane, 2006. The former head of the World Bank looks at a raft of examples of how countries have developed since the end of the Second World War and offers suggestions for improving the process.

Friedman, M., *Capitalism and Freedom*, University of Chicago Press, 1962. The monetarist on the connection between competitive capitalism and political freedom.

Bell, D., *Coming of Post-Industrial Society: Venture in Social Forecasting*, Basic Books, 1974.

Amin, A. (ed.), *Post-Fordism: A Reader*, Wiley Blackwell, 1994.

Friedman, J. (ed.), *What Caused the Financial Crisis*, University of Pennsylvania Press, 2011.

Epstein, G.A. (ed.), *Financialization and the World Economy*, Edward Elgar Publishing, 2005.

Haskel, J. & Westlake, S., *Capitalism Without Capital: The Rise of the Intangible Economy*. Princeton University Press, 2017.

Piketty, T., *Capital in the Twenty-First Century*, Harvard University Press, 2014.

Bjørnholt, M. & McKay, A. (eds.), *Counting on Marilyn Waring: New Advances in Feminist Economics (2nd edition)*, Demeter Press, 2014.

Waring, M., *Counting for Nothing: What Men Value and What Women Are Worth*, University of Toronto Press, 1999.

Mies, M., *Patriarchy and Accumulation on a World Scale: Women in the International Division of Labour*, Zed Books, 1986.

Warsh, D., *Knowledge and the Wealth of Nations: A Story of Economic Discovery*, W.W. Norton & Company, 2007.

Acknowledgements

The artist would like to thank Duncan Heath and the guys at the Oporto cafe and dedicate this book to Silvina and all the people who suffer around the globe in consequence of greed.

Dan Cryan has degrees in philosophy from UCL and now works at the intersection of media and technology in California.

Sharron Shatil is a philosophy and political thought lecturer at the Open University in Israel.

Piero is an illustrator, artist and graphic designer whose work has twice been included in the Royal College of Art exhibition in London.

Index